D0105844

P
236
.C57
1983

84-1259/0166 ✓

DATE DUE

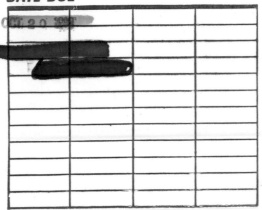

TEXAS WOMAN'S UNIVERSITY
LIBRARY
DENTON, TEXAS

DEMCO

CV PHONOLOGY

Linguistic Inquiry Monographs
Samuel Jay Keyser, general editor

Errata Sheet: CV Phonology

page 12, the first line after Figure 7: change "V" to "vowel"

8th line after Figure 7: insert "V is not preceded by tautosyllabic V and" between "where" and "X"

page 16, replace Figure 12 by the following:

Figure 12

page 17, replace Figure 13c by the following:

c. nucleus display

$$C \quad C \quad \overset{\nu}{\underset{\wedge}{V}} \quad C \quad C$$

page 31, three lines before Figure 7: change "(8a)" to "(7a)"

page 85, third line of the second paragraph: change "identical" to "adjacent"

page 85, fourth line of the second paragraph: change "within" to "within words"

page 90, Figure 38b should be replaced by the following:

b. A V-initial syllable constitutes the left branch of a foot only if it is phrase initial; otherwise, it is a member of the same foot as the preceding syllable.

(continues overleaf)

page 103, replace Figure 58b and 58c by the following:

b. extrasyllabic consonants or consonant sequences occurring finally in noun and verb stems (roots plus any derivational endings) undergo obligatory truncation in the lexicon.

c. only word final consonants or consonant sequences may be extrasyllabic.

page 104, fourth line: change "undergo truncation" to "show alternation in liason contexts"

page 127, first line of Figure 19a: change "sinamstnank" to "sinəmstə́nk"

page 148, last line of text: change "/pa/" to "/ga/"

page 161, last line before Figure 37: change "*sosə:yá:q́a:" to "*sosə:yó:q́a:"

third line of Figure 37: change "yá:q́" to "yó:q́"

page 162, first line Figure 39: change "show" to "shows"

page 184, first line: change "pronunciation" to "prononciation"

page 187, third line of the fifth bibliographical entry: change "D1 D12" to "D1-D12"

CV PHONOLOGY
A Generative Theory of the Syllable

George N. Clements
Samuel Jay Keyser

The MIT Press
Cambridge, Massachusetts
London, England

This volume was computer composed by the authors using facilities made available by the Center for Cognitive Science, the Research Laboratory of Electronics, the Department of Electrical Engineering and Computer Science and the Artificial Intelligence Laboratory at MIT. The volume was prepared in this fashion in order to reduce costs to the publisher and, ultimately, to the purchaser. The sophistication of the formating programs has made it possible to replicate letterpress style to a considerable degree so that the quality of the output compares favorably with more familiar but more costly modes of printing. The authors would like to express their gratitude to the above organizations for making this mode of book production possible.

© 1983 by The Massachusetts Institute of Technology

All rights reserved. No part of this book may be reproduced in any form or by any means, electronic or mechanical, including photocopying, recording, or by any information storage and retrieval system, without permission in writing from the publisher.

This book was printed and bound in the United States of America.

Library of Congress Cataloging in Publication Data

Clements, George N.
  CV phonology.

  (Linguistic inquiry monographs ; 9)
  Supersedes 2 earlier studies by the authors:
A three-tiered theory of the syllable (1981) and The hierarchical nature of the Klamath syllable (priv. circulated 1980).
  Bibliography: p.
  1. Grammar, Comparative and general—Syllable. 2. Grammar, Comparative and general—Phonology. 3. Generative grammar. I. Keyser, Samuel Jay, 1935– . II. Title. III. Title; C.V. phonology.
IV. Series.
P236.C57 1983   415   83–10669
ISBN 0–262–03098–5
ISBN 0–262–53047–3 (pbk.)

TEXAS WOMAN'S UNIVERSITY LIBRARY

Table of Contents

Foreword

We are pleased to present this monograph as the ninth in the series *Linguistic Inquiry Monographs*. These monographs will present new and original research beyond the scope of the article. Because of their originality it is hoped that they will benefit our field by bringing to it perspectives that will stimulate further research and insight.

Originally published in a limited edition, the *Linguistic Inquiry Monograph* series is now available on a much wider scale. This change is due to the great interest engendered by the series and the needs of a growing readership. The editors wish to thank the readers for their support and welcome suggestions about future directions the series might take.

Samuel Jay Keyser
for the Editorial Board

Acknowledgments

The present work introduces a new approach to syllable representation. Minimally extending the hierarchical approach developed by D. Kahn in his 1976 MIT dissertation, it proposes an additional tier in phonological representation - the CV-tier - which defines functional positions within the syllable, as well as allowing a simple account of such syllable-related phenomena as length, complex segments, syllable weight, compensatory lengthening and the mora.

This monograph incorporates two earlier studies by the authors. The first three chapters comprise a substantially revised version of "A Three-tiered Theory of the Syllable," published in 1981 as <u>Occasional Paper No. 19 of the Center for Cognitive Science</u> at MIT. The last two chapters are based upon our "The Hierarchical Nature of the Klamath Syllable", privately circulated in 1980, which has been entirely rewritten for this volume. The present work supersedes these earlier studies.

The authors would like to thank Morris Halle and Elizabeth Selkirk for invaluable advice and criticism of earlier versions of this monograph. Their friendly, yet incisive comment has influenced the final shape of our work in important ways. Our debt to John McCarthy extends beyond that already acknowledged in the text which follows to include useful discussion of the material. In this regard we are also indebted to Alan Prince for his pointed commentary in discussion with one of the authors. Annie Rialland has been extremely helpful as have been the written responses to our distribution of an early version of this work from John Goldsmith, Bruce Hayes, Larry Hyman and Karin Michelson.

The authors would like to acknowledge their great debt to Per-Kristian Halvorsen and Meg Withgott for their expertise and advice. The programming facilities through which this manuscript was prepared, including the special symbols repertoire and the formating setup, are due entirely to them. Without these aids, the preparation of this manuscript in its present format would not have been possible.

This work was supported in part by a grant to the Center for Cognitive Science at MIT by the Sloan Foundation under its Particular Program in Cognitive Science.

CV PHONOLOGY

Chapter 1: Overview

Until very recently, generative phonology was premised on the notion that phonological representation consists of linear strings of segments with no hierarchical organization other than that provided by syntactic phrase structure. In particular, the notion syllable was thought to play no role in phonological organization. However, there has been increasing evidence that the exclusion of the syllable is a serious omission in generative phonology and that many phonological rules only receive appropriate formulation in terms of this notion. As a consequence some generative phonologists have proposed to integrate the syllable into revised versions of phonological theory.

What considerations have motivated the renewed interest in the syllable in current generative phonology? In our view, innovations in scientific theories involve two factors. The first is the identification of serious empirical inadequacies in the current research paradigm. The second is the perhaps independent development of new models which offer the possibility of treating well-known problems from a new perspective. In fact, both of these conditions have been fulfilled in the recent history of phonology.

One of the first examples of the empirical inadequacies of linear systems of generative phonology stemmed from the need to recognize a distinction between "weak" and "strong" clusters in the system of English stress (Chomsky and Halle 1968). In terms of the standard model of phonology, this distinction could not be derived directly from properties of formal phonological representation. Hence, Chomsky and Halle provided an informal, "unofficial" characterization of this distinction, defining it in terms of certain sets of substrings particular to English. In terms of this approach, the distinction between "weak" and "strong" clusters was an arbitrary property of English phonology.[1] Moreover, this distinction could not be related to the configurations which were involved in other rules of English phonology. For example, one would have to define different and equally arbitrary configurations to characterize the environment of such rules as flap formation, glottalization, r-deletion, and the like (see Kahn 1976). It is apparent that such an approach, if extended to other languages, would give an overly generous margin of freedom to the phonologist attempting to discover the significant generalizations governing the language under investigation.

With regard to the second point, work by Williams (1976), Goldsmith (1974,1976), Liberman (1975), Liberman and Prince (1977) and others in entirely independent areas of phonology led to the development of models in which certain properties of utterances, such as tone and stress, were represented in terms of features or feature configurations extracted from the linear string of phonemes and arrayed on independent levels of representation. Given the ability of such approaches to provide satisfactory solutions to problems that had previously proven intractable, it was natural and appropriate that phonologists should consider the possibility of extending these approaches to new problem areas.

Under the stimulus of such work, several phonologists have offered compelling arguments for recognizing the syllable as a hierarchical unit in phonological representation. Important recent contributions include those of Kahn (1976), Selkirk (1978), McCarthy (1979a), Kiparsky (1979), Halle and Vergnaud (1979) and Leben (1980), among others. Despite widespread agreement on the basic approach, however, there is considerable divergence of opinion as to the nature of the hierarchical structure required.

---

1. This problem was noted by Chomsky and Halle (1968) themselves. They commented on it as follows: "We recall that we were forced to include the "weak cluster" option not only in the Main Stress Rule and Tensing Rules, but also in the Auxiliary Reduction Rule... As noted, this repetition indicates that we have failed to capture important properties of strong and weak clusters and thus points to a defect in our theory that merits further attention." (p.241, fn. 3).

Fundamental questions that remain to be answered include the following. How many tiers or levels of representation are involved between the root node of the syllable and the terminal segments that it dominates? Is there a fixed number of such tiers or are they in principle unbounded? Are syllable trees binary branching or n-ary branching? Are the nodes of hierarchical trees labelled? If so, what are the appropriate categories? How are entities of the several tiers related to one another? Along what parameters may languages vary in their selection of alternative syllable structures?

Our point of departure in the present work is the hierarchical theory of the syllable introduced by Kahn in his influential thesis <u>Syllable-based Generalizations in English Phonology</u> (1976). In this study Kahn proposed to extend the notion of phonological representation assumed in such works as Chomsky and Halle's <u>The Sound Pattern of English</u> (1968) by introducing a new tier of representation involving strings of the symbol <u>S</u>, representing the node "syllable". These nodes are linked to segments (single column feature matrices) by association lines of the type proposed in autosegmental phonology. Each maximal sequence of segments dominated by a single node <u>S</u> constitutes a syllable, as shown in the following representation of the word <u>Jennifer</u>:

Figure 1

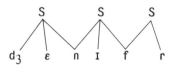

Certain properties can be extracted from this mode of representation. First, by counting the number of <u>S</u>'s on the upper tier, we see that the word <u>Jennifer</u> consists of three syllables. Moreover, we know that the three syllables in question consist of the sequences dʒɛn, nɪf and fr. A further feature of Kahn's representations is the fact that certain segments may be ambisyllabic in the sense that they are dominated by two elements of the upper tier. Thus, in Jennifer the n and the f are both characterized as ambisyllabic.

Kahn's work provided a convincing demonstration of the theoretical advantages of recognizing the syllable as a hierarchical unit. In particular, he showed that a number of productive, low-level processes in English phonology interact with each other in intricate ways that resolved themselves into a small number of simple statements. He clearly demonstrated that linear alternatives were inherently incapable of giving equally satisfactory results.

Not unexpectedly, there were a number of issues which remained unresolved in this ground-breaking thesis. For example, Kahn's specification of the English syllable failed to provide a characterization of the notions "possible initial cluster" and "possible final cluster". Kahn's assumption that the set of syllable initial clusters was coextensive with the set of word initial clusters was incorrect as a universal claim. Further, his theory did not specify the point in phonological derivations where syllable-building rules first apply. Recent research, moreover, has suggested that there is need not only to build syllables but also to rebuild them at later points in a derivation, following the operation of certain kinds of rules such as vowel deletion and vowel epenthesis; Kahn, of course, had no occasion to consider resyllabification since the phenomena he examined did not motivate such processes. Finally, Kahn's hierarchical mode of representation was insufficiently rich in that it did not distinguish syllable peaks from marginal elements. For example, consider a syllable consisting of the sequence /rl/, a possible representation of the English word earl. In Kahn's mode of representation, these two segments are dominated by a single node S. It is impossible to tell from the tree configuration alone that it is the r rather than the l that constitutes the syllable peak. In order to make such distinctions, Kahn assigned the feature [+syllabic] to one terminal element of each syllable and the feature [-syllabic] to the others. However, as a number of phoneticians have pointed out, syllabicity is not an intrinsic characteristic of segments but rather involves the relationship between a segment and its neighbors on either side. In accord with this fact, it might be proposed that the syllabicity or non-syllabicity of a segment is more aptly characterized in terms of its position in a syllable tree.

One point on which there has been a convergence of opinion in the more recent literature is that in a more highly enriched theory of the syllable, syllable trees are binary branching. Earlier we raised the question of the number of levels that intervene between the segment and the root node. The binary branching theory holds that there is no upper limit on the number of such levels. Rather, the depth of branching is determined by the number of terminal elements in the syllable.

Although we are convinced that more structure must be postulated than Kahn was willing to recognize, it proves hard to motivate the rich structure required under the binary branching tree hypothesis. In particular, less constrained versions of this hypothesis present the language learner with the problem of selecting among a variety of possible branching structures for the syllable structures of his or her language. For example, consider a syllable of the form CV. It is clear by inspection that there is only one possible tree that can be constructed over this string. The choice of alternatives increases with strings of the length CVC, where the number of possible binary trees is two. If the string contains four segments as in CVCC, the number of possible trees increases to five:

Figure 2

A string of five segments as in CCVCC can accommodate 14 different binary branching trees; a string of six segments will accommodate 42; seven segments yield 132; eight segments yield 469; nine segments yield 1430; ten segments yield 4862 and so on.[2] It is clear that an unconstrained binary branching theory provides a far greater number of possible trees than are ever utilized in natural language. The conclusion that one is led to is that the theory is, from this point of view, in need of substantive constraint. Notice, however, that any such constraint must be stipulated in the theory. There has been no agreement in the literature to date as to the nature of the appropriate stipulations.

Another problem arises when we consider how the distinction between "heavy" and "light" syllables should be characterized in terms of binary branching trees. It has long been noted that in many languages, prosodic rules treat alike syllables containing the following sequences: V: (long vowel), VG (diphthong), VC (short vowel plus consonant). Such heavy syllables contrast with light syllables, which end in single short vowels (cf. Kurytowicz 1948). In systems of this type, for example, the hypothetical syllable [pa:] would be prosodically equivalent to the syllable [pam]. In order to express this equivalence a binary branching theory might propose the following representations:[3]

---

2. This series constitutes what is known to mathematicians as a Catalan series. The function which determines this series has been worked out independently by John Goldsmith and by George Boolos, to whom we express our thanks. For a discussion of this series in terms of prepositional phrase attachment and conjunction in English, see Martin, Church and Patil (1981). See, also, Church and Patil (1982).

3. Such representations are discussed in Kiparsky (1981) and in Ingria (1980). We know of no alternative proposals for providing unitary characterizations of heavy syllables in universal phonology. See, however, Selkirk (1980) for a somewhat different proposal for English and Harris (1983) for an alternative proposal for Spanish.

Figure 3

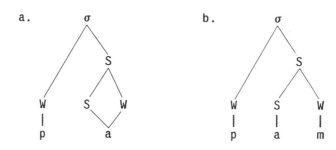

The equivalence of these two syllable types is expressed at the level of hierarchical structure where, in each case, the S dominated by the root node dominates the sequence SW. Given this identity, one would expect the relevant terminal sequences in (3) to behave alike with respect to phonological rules sensitive to syllable weight, a prediction which is, in fact, correct, as noted above.

But consider now longer syllables, similar to those above but with a consonant added to the right:

Figure 4

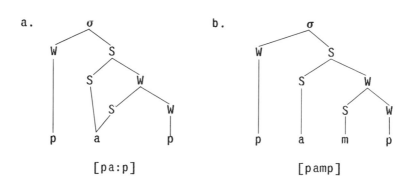

Here, too, the tree captures the structural equivalence of the terminal substrings [a:p] and [amp]: both are exhaustively dominated by an S which is immediately dominated by the root node σ and which immediately dominates

SW. However, notice that there is a difference between the long vowel in (4a) and that in (3a). In (3a), the long vowel [a:] is a single constituent immediately dominated by the sequence SW. Consequently, it is described as a single unit that occupies successively strong and weak positions in syllable structure. In (4), on the other hand, the long vowel [a:] is no longer a constituent and is immediately dominated by the sequence SS, rather than SW. Thus, the same terminal sequence is treated as having two distinct structures depending upon whether or not it is final in the syllable. A theory characterizing long vowels as in (3a) and (4a) claims that such vowels might exhibit phonologically different behavior purely by virtue of their different hierarchical structure. To the best of our knowledge no examples of such a distinction exist. Similarly, we know of no evidence that the terminal strings [am] of (3b) and (4b) behave differently by virtue of their different hierarchical structure. This suggests that an adequate phonological theory should provide a uniform characterization of the notions "heavy" and "light" syllable.

In this study we wish to explore a new approach to the syllable. In this theory, which minimally extends the framework of Kahn (1976), we introduce a third tier in syllable representation which mediates between the syllable tier and the segmental tier and which we call the CV-tier. In this approach Jennifer will be represented as follows:

Figure 5

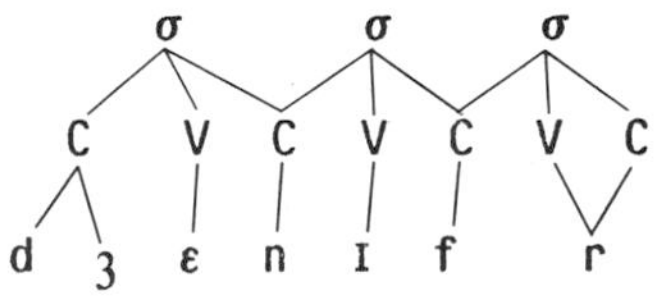

The elements of the CV-tier distinguish between syllable peaks and syllable non-peaks (or syllable margins). Specifically, any segment dominated by V is interpreted as a syllable peak, and any segment dominated only by C is interpreted as a non-peak. Thus in (5), the terminal elements [ɛ, ɪ, r] constitute syllable peaks; the remaining elements are non-peaks. Given this account of syllabicity, the old feature [+syllabic] can be dispensed with.[4] Since the major thrust of the present work is to motivate the CV-tier in phonological theory, we leave more detailed discussion of its character until later. Here, however, we note that the branching relationships between adjacent levels in this theory may not only be one-to-many, but also many-to-one, as shown in (5).

The notion of the CV-tier is not a new one in phonology. In traditional and structuralist theories, canonic constraints on the structure of certain units were frequently formulated in terms of strings of the abstract units C and V; for an early statement see Hockett (1947). Similarly, the conception of the syllable developed in Abercrombie (1967) draws heavily upon statements involving these units. What is different about the status of C and V units in the present theory is that they are regarded not as variables belonging exclusively to the vocabulary of phonological description, but as entities of formal phonological representation separate from consonants and vowels and arrayed on independent lines or tiers as shown in (5). The usefulness of such units in phonological representation was first suggested in work by Thráinsson (1978) on Icelandic preaspiration and Menn (1977, 1978) on child language acquisition. However, it was in the quite independent work of McCarthy on Semitic word formation (1979b, 1981, in press) that the place of these units in linguistic theory was most thoroughly established. Our work, as will be apparent, is greatly indebted to McCarthy's careful and persuasive studies, which have been complemented by the work

---

4. Notice that once we have eliminated the feature [+syllabic], vowels and glides are distinguished only by whether they are dominated by C or V on the CV-tier. For further treatment of this matter see Chapter 4, and especially section 4.3.5.

Obviously the elimination of the feature [+syllabic] will have important consequences for feature theory. In particular, it will impinge upon familiar accounts of French consonant truncation and liaison which have been cited as evidence for the feature [+syllabic] (cf. Chomsky and Halle 1968, pp. 353-55). We return to this in Chapter 3, section 8.

of Halle and Vergnaud (1980), Harris (1980), and others.

However, our use of the units C and V differs from McCarthy's conception in one important respect. McCarthy recognized the independent status of the CV-tier in classical Arabic in large part on the basis of the fact that certain CV-sequences function as independent morphemes in this language. McCarthy termed such morphemes prosodic templates. Indeed, this evidence provided some of the most striking support for McCarthy's analyses and forms the basis of his theory of nonconcatenative morphology.

In this study we turn to evidence from quite a different area, that of syllable phonology. We provide evidence for the view that the CV-tier is a component of syllable representation regardless of its functioning in the word formation component. Although much recent research has already demonstrated the value of pursuing this view, we believe that the full range of evidence supporting the recognition of the CV-tier in phonological representation has not yet been brought to light, and that the consequences of the CV-tier for syllable theory have not been fully appreciated. In this study we offer a unified framework which draws upon and receives motivation from phonological as well as morphological evidence.

In the view we present below, the CV-tier is not only, or even primarily, a constituent of morphological analysis, but serves in phonological representation to distinguish functional positions within the syllable. In McCarthy's model the distinction between "C" and "V" was, strictly speaking, redundant, since this distinction could be independently determined from the hierarchical syllable structure (involving binary branching and S/W labelling) imposed on the CV-tier. In the present theory the distinction between "C" and "V" is no longer redundant since the units of the CV-tier themselves define functional positions (peak versus nonpeak) within the syllable. In this respect the CV-tier can be seen as subsuming the function of the earlier feature category [syllabic]. However, the elements of the CV-tier are not merely analogues of the features [+syllabic] and

[-syllabic], but serve the additional and equally important function of defining the primitive units of timing at the sub-syllabic level of phonological representation. In particular, it appears as if the useful but ill-defined notion of "phonological segment" can best be reconstructed at this level. Thus, we will show that what are normally regarded as single segments (both simple and complex) correspond to single instances of C or V on the CV-tier while geminate or bimoric sequences correspond to two units of the CV-tier. Where the correspondence between traditional usage and CV-representation is not exact, as in the case of "long" vowels and consonants (often treated as single segments), it seems that the representations offered by the present theory provide the more useful basis for phonological description. We return to a closer examination of these matters in the following chapters.

Let us turn now to the set of questions raised earlier, and ask, in particular, whether a three-tiered model of the syllable is sufficiently rich to provide for a complete characterization of all statements and processes referring to the syllable and its constituents, or whether further hierarchical structure should be recognized. Many writers of the past (Trubetzkoy 1958, Pike and Pike 1947, Haugen 1956) and present (Selkirk 1978, Halle and Vergnaud 1980) have proposed a further set of constituents smaller than the syllable, taking consonant and vowel segments as their members. These constituents may be termed the onset, nucleus and coda. Under such proposals, the word stout might be represented, in part, as follows:

Figure 6

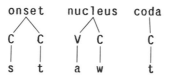

There is a certain amount of evidence suggesting that the category "nucleus" plays a role in phonological organization. This evidence consists of its role in defining the distinction between heavy and light syllables mentioned earlier. We observed that a heavy syllable ends in a long vowel, a diphthong, or else a short vowel followed by a consonant, while a light syllable ends in a single short vowel. Let us assume that long vowels are universally represented by means of the multi-attachment of a single vowel matrix to two positions on the CV-tier, as follows:

Figure 7

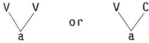

As this figure shows, the units dominating the V matrix may consist of the sequence VV or the sequence VC. The choice between these two depends upon language specific considerations that will be elaborated upon in Chapters 3 and 5.

The notions light syllable and heavy syllable may be formally defined in terms of the category "nucleus", where we take the nucleus to be a prosodic category consisting of any and all tautosyllabic sequences of the form V(X), where X ranges over single occurrences of C and V. Light syllables are those containing a simple (non-branching) nucleus, that is V, while heavy syllables are those containing a complex (branching) nucleus, that is VV or VC.[5]

---

5. Note that this definition precludes language particular restrictions on the membership of the nucleus. In all languages, any and all tautosyllabic sequences of the form VV or VC, regardless of the nature of the segmental matrices they dominate, constitute nuclei in our sense of this term.

Figure 8

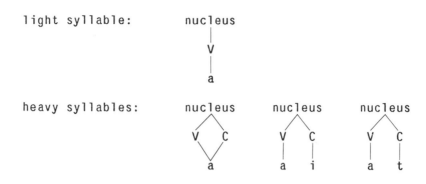

We may now return to the commonly observed fact that the phonological systems of many languages are sensitive to the distinction between heavy and light syllables. As one example, recall that the stress rules of English distinguish between what have been termed "weak" and "strong" clusters, as shown in the bracketed portions of the following words:

Figure 9

weak cluster: Amer[ĭc]a

strong clusters: Wisc[ŏns]in

Ariz[ō n]a

A "weak cluster" in Chomsky and Halle's account consisted of a single short vowel followed by no more than one consonant (or else by one of certain clusters such as /pl/, /tr/, /kw/, etc.). A "strong cluster" consisted of a short vowel followed by two or more consonants (not including the set of clusters just mentioned), or else of a long (tense) vowel plus zero or more consonants. In terms of syllable representations, we may reformulate this distinction as one between heavy and light syllables (as indicated in brackets):

Figure 10

light syllable: V
                                            |
                                      Ame[ri]ca

heavy syllables: VC
                                           ||
                                     Wis[con]sin

                                          V C
                                           \/
                                     Ari[zo]na

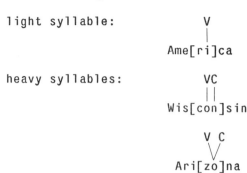

The rules for assigning regular stress in English words are sensitive to this distinction, as well as to the distinction between short and long vowels. Thus, the familiar rule for assigning main stress to nouns of three syllables or more, illustrated in the above examples, places stress on the rightmost syllable that is not a final short-vowel syllable or a penultimate light syllable.

It will be noticed that in this and other rules that are sensitive to syllable weight, it is normally just the internal structure of the nucleus that is relevant; the internal structure of the onset and coda are usually irrelevant. Thus, for example, the syllables r˘ıs and tr˘ıs are equivalent in the operation of English stress rules, just as are the syllables r¯o and r¯ot. This generalization can easily be formulated if the nucleus is a unit in phonological representation to which rules of stress assignment have privileged access. [6]

---

6. Our formulation does not imply that stress rules may not have access to segments lying outside of the nucleus. Roca (1982) provides evidence from Spanish to suggest that the onset plays a role in stress assignment. In that language antepenultimate stress is excluded under two conditions: first, when the penultimate syllable is heavy; second, when the final syllable begins with one of the following set of consonants: ñ, ll, ch, j, y, rr. If all of these consonants were derivable from clusters, it would be possible to eliminate the second constraint since the first member of the cluster would close the preceding syllable making it heavy. However, of these consonants, only the last can be derived synchronically from a cluster. The former derive historically from clusters but must be analyzed as single consonants synchronically. Thus the second of the two constraints cannot be eliminated, and shows that stress rules may involve crucial reference to elements lying outside the nucleus, in this case in syllable initial position.

We have so far proposed that the nucleus is a category of prosodic organization dependent on, but formally distinct from the syllable, and we have argued that the distinction between "light" and "heavy" syllables can be accommodated in terms of a distinction between simple and branching nuclei. But what of the formal status of the other categories represented in (6), that is, the "onset" and the "coda"?

As far as we have been able to determine, there is no linguistic evidence suggesting that phonological rules ever make crucial reference to the categories "onset" and "coda". Thus, it appears that the set of syllable structure conditions defining the set of well-formed syllables for each language can be stated with complete adequacy with reference to the categories "syllable" and "nucleus". For example, the distinction between initial consonant clusters and final consonant clusters, which are subject to independent constraints, can be characterized directly with reference to the brackets which delimit the boundaries of the syllable. The distinction between constraints holding of consonant clusters and constraints holding of long vowels or diphthongs can be characterized with reference to the CV-tier. An account of the well-formed initial clusters in English, following these principles, will be given in Chapter 2.

Moreover, it turns out that many rules of the phonology would have to be complicated in unenlightening ways if the onset and coda were constituents of the syllable. For example, consider a rule having the effect of affiliating a syllable-final consonant to a following vowel-initial syllable. This rule defines the following operation, as long as we assume that the onset and coda are not constituents of the syllable:

Figure 11

$$
\begin{array}{cc}
\sigma \quad \sigma & \sigma \quad \sigma \\
| \quad | \quad \text{---}\!\!> & \diagup\!\!| \\
C \quad V & C \quad V
\end{array}
$$

We may state the rule formally as follows, using the abbreviatory conventions of autosegmental phonology:

Figure 12

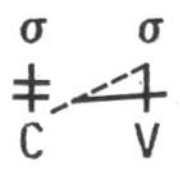

σ   σ

C   V

Without belaboring the point, it is clear that the presence of intermediate constituents like "onset" and "coda" would introduce undesirable formal complications into the statement of such rules which at best would necessitate the introduction of interpretative conventions or the like to eliminate them. Such complications are not necessary in a theory which does not postulate the categories "onset" and "coda" in the first place.

On the basis of these considerations we propose the following minimal enrichment of the three-tiered theory of syllable structure developed so far. We suggest that phonological representation involves, in addition to the σ-tier, the CV-tier and the segmental tier, a further tier which we term the nucleus tier, consisting of strings of the symbol *v* linked to at least one, and at most two elements of the CV-tier as explained above.

Let us use the term display to refer to any partial phonological representation consisting of two or three autosegmentally related tiers. A full phonological representation may thus be understood as a set of such displays, in which the CV-tier may occur more than once. In this sense the CV-tier may be thought of as the "skeleton" of a phonological representation, to use the term suggested by Halle and Vergnaud (1980).

Returning to our earlier example, the phonological representation of the word stout will contain the following displays. We use conventional alphabetical symbols to represent the units of the segmental tier.[7]

Figure 13

a. segmental display

```
C C V C C
| | | | |
s t a w t
```

b. syllable display

c. nucleus display

In this conception, the nucleus display (13c) forms a different "plane" from the syllable display (13b). In other words, the nucleus is not a subconstituent of the syllable, but forms an independent prosodic unit on a separate plane of representation. This gives us, in effect, a nucleus "projection" in the sense of Halle and Vergnaud (1979). For expository convenience, we will also make use of three-tiered displays consisting of two-dimensional conflations of two-tiered displays sharing a tier in common. The three-tiered displays given below will be of particular significance in our later discussion of phonological processes. We call the first a "three-tiered syllable display" and the second a "three-tiered nucleus display".

---

7. The segmental tier may very well be a composite formed from several independent tiers, such as the laryngeal tier, the nasal tier, and others. We will not be concerned with the internal structure of the segmental tier in this work.

Figure 14

A further distinction can be drawn between the elements of the σ-tier, the CV-tier and the nucleus tier, on the one hand, and the elements of certain other tiers, such as the segmental tier and the tonal tier on the other. The former, unlike the latter, are not defined in terms of phonetic features with specifiable physical correlates but are rather structural units, representing the higher-level serial organization of speech units that appears to be a general characteristic of linguistic structure at all levels: syntactic, semantic and phonetic. We may refer to these tiers and certain others (for example, the μ-tier or morpheme tier (McCarthy, 1981) and the F-tier, or foot-tier (see Chapter 3.7)) collectively as <u>structural tiers</u> as opposed to <u>phonetic tiers</u>. A complete phonological representation, then, consists of a composite representation containing both structural tiers and phonetic tiers.

It should be clear, even from this preliminary discussion, that certain advantages follow from this approach in contrast to the binary branching approach outlined earlier. For example, the problem of analytical indeterminacy resulting from the proliferation of syllable types disappears in the present theory, since, given any sequence of CV-elements constituting a syllable, there is only one way of constructing the syllable display. Furthermore, we have seen that the distinction between heavy and light syllables does not raise problems for the representation of vowel length, as it did in one particular version of the binary branching theory. In the theory presented here, heavy and light syllables are characterized as in (8). As a result, long vowels in the syllables [paː] and [paːp] are given a uniform representation:

Figure 15

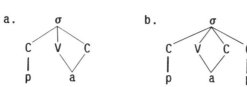

A question not yet touched on is whether the theory of the syllable should recognize further units of structure such as the rhyme (or rime), comprising the nucleus and all following segments within the syllable. Notice that the present theory can be extended in a very simple manner to accommodate such an additional unit, by recognizing a further tier, the rhyme-tier:

Figure 16

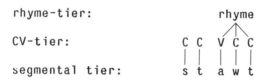

Given the units of representation developed so far, it turns out to be hard to find fully persuasive evidence for this additional tier. We consider some possible evidence here.

In the first place, there have occasionally been claims to the effect that syllable structure conditions never involve distributional constraints holding between the nucleus and preceding elements, while, on the other hand, they frequently are found to express cooccurrence restrictions between the nucleus and following elements. For example, Fudge (1969, 272-3) argues that in English, "certain Peaks do not cooccur with certain Codas...while there is no such constraint between Onset and Peak."   (In Fudge's terminology the Peak is defined as the position that may be occupied by a vowel or diphthong.) This observation, it might be argued, would follow from a theory in which syllable structure conditions only held within subconstituents of the syllable. In this case, the onset/rhyme division would constitute an absolute barrier to cooccurrence restrictions. However, this observation is not generally correct: cooccurrence restrictions holding between the nucleus and preceding elements of the syllable appear to be just as common as cooccurrence restrictions holding between the nucleus and following elements. Consider, for example, the following from English:

Figure 17

a. In dialects distinguishing /aː/ from /ɒː/, the sequence /waː/ is excluded. Exceptions are limited to a few loans from French which are usually "regularized" by English speakers: reservoir, memoir, voyeur.

b. Anterior fricatives /f,v,s,z,θ,δ/ are excluded before /uːr/.

c. Voiced fricatives and /Cl/ clusters are excluded before /ʊ/.

d. /vuː/ is excluded, except in voodoo, a rhyming adaptation from Ewe vodu (cf. the regular French form vaudou [vodu]), and in the French loan rendez-vous.

e. Stop plus /w/ clusters are excluded before /uː, ʊ, ʌ, aw/: *kwuːt, etc.

f. /Cr/ clusters are excluded before /er,or,ar/: *trair, etc.

g. /Cl/ clusters are excluded before /V̆l/ and, indeed, before / V̄ l/ with the single exception of flail.

h. As pointed out by Browne (1981), English has virtually no words consisting of the form $sC_aV̆C_a$, that is, s, a consonant, a short vowel, and the consonant again; as Browne observes, "this fact is astonishing when we think of how many short-vowel monosyllables the language does have." The only exceptions have /t/ as C_a: stet (a proofreader's term) from Latin; stat (a local slang term for statistics); and Stitt (in Sonny Stitt, the name of a well-known musician). Moreover, our search through the 20,000 entries of the 1964 edition of the Merriam-Webster Pocket Dictionary reveals only three items in which /sCV̆C/ appears as a word internal syllable; namely, rheostat, thermostat and sextet. Notice that in these exceptions as well, /t/ appears as C_a. This constraint has persisted from Anglo-Saxon times, when the only known exception (once again with /t/) was stot 'a kind of horse'.

A few of these constraints could, perhaps, be regarded as accidental gaps, but not all of them can be. English is by no means unusual in having constraints holding between initial and nuclear members of the syllable. For example, in Klamath, a language we discuss in more detail in Chapters 4 and 5, the only syllable structure constraint is one excluding the sequence /yi/.

A second argument for the rhyme constituent could be based upon languages which impose an upper limit on the length of the rhyme. The claim here would be that the rhyme furnishes the most appropriate domain for the statement of such a constraint. For example, in Turkish we find that syllables may contain long vowels or short vowels. Short vowel syllables, but not long vowel syllables, may end in a consonant cluster: <u>raks</u> 'dance', <u>aʃk</u> 'love'. Notice further that while both <u>aks</u> and <u>aʃk</u> are acceptable rhymes, we find no longer rhymes such as *<u>aʃks</u>. These constraints could be stated as follows: Turkish permits no four-member rhymes. On the other hand, these constraints follow equally well from an analysis available under the present theory. We might assume that final consonant clusters ending in /s/ do not belong to the level of core syllable representation in Turkish but are formed by a later rule of s-affiliation, which affiliates /s/ to an immediately preceding nucleus. This rule will permit the adjunction of /s/ to the sequence /ak/ to form /aks/, but will prohibit the adjunction of /s/ to a sequence like /aʃk/, where the final segment lies outside of the nucleus. While we cannot defend this particular account of Turkish in detail here, we will show independent motivation for affiliation rules of this type in another language, Klamath, in Chapter 4.

A third type of potential evidence for the rhyme constituent might be drawn from "external evidence" such as speech errors, word games and the like. While it has sometimes been proposed that this evidence argues unambiguously for the grouping of the nucleus together with following elements in the syllable into a single constituent, the facts are rather more complicated. For example, while the nucleus and post-nuclear elements can be seen to behave as a unit in many English speech errors, so can the nucleus and pre-nuclear elements. Fromkin (1971) cites the following: <u>pussy cat</u> → <u>cassy put</u>; <u>lost and found</u> → <u>faust and lawned</u>; <u>stress and pitch</u> → <u>piss and stretch</u>. As far as word games are concerned, languages for which onset/rhyme organization has been proposed on other grounds may have word games that require grouping the nucleus and the onset together as a unit. An example is the Finnish word game reported on in Campbell (1980) in which "the first consonant and vowel of each succeeding pair of words are interchanged" (p.247). Thus, we find the following examples:

Figure 18

saksalaisia hätyytettiin → häksäläisiä satuutettiin 'The Germans were attacked.'

tykkään urheilusta → ukkaan tyrheilystä 'I like sports.'

(Note that the vowel changes are due to vowel harmony.) Evidence from word games, therefore, cannot be taken as unequivocal evidence for syllable organization.[8]

We conclude that while the nucleus may be grouped together with following elements frequently in speech errors, word games and the like, groupings of the nucleus with preceding elements are sufficiently common as to rule out any theory forming a constituent out of the first pair and not the second. Two conclusions are possible: either both groupings must be recognized and, in the present theory, constitute two new structural tiers at the level of lexical representation, or else neither grouping should be recognized. Due to the apparent absence of any language internal evidence for the first of these positions, we are forced to draw the latter conclusion.

A final argument for the rhyme might involve rhyming traditions in English and other languages. It has been maintained (though not, as far as we know, in print) that the poetic notion "rhyme" is appropriately defined in terms of the linguistic category "rhyme". In fact, however, it is amply clear that the poetic device is quite different from the linguistic notion "rhyme". Consider, for instance, Chaucer's famous rhyme in the Prologue to The

---

8. Consistent with this view is the discussion in Yip (1982) showing that Chinese word games provide evidence for the CV-tier but do not provide evidence for onset/rhyme organization.

<u>Canterbury Tales</u>, namely <u>cinamome: to me</u> (with primary stress on the penultimate syllable of each member), or such Modern English pairs as <u>sinister: minister</u> or <u>higgledy: piggledy</u>. In all such cases the rhyme depends upon the identity of the final stressed vowel and the entire string to its right within the word or verse line, including, crucially, all intervocalic consonants. In such pairs, there is clearly no single constituent which uniquely defines the notion rhyme.

The theory which we present in the following chapters represents an attempt to achieve maximal theoretical simplicity in the face of data of considerable intricacy and variety. Wherever possible, we have tried to avoid unnecessary additions to the theoretical apparatus of phonological theory by making maximal use of the notational distinctions provided by three-tiered syllable structures. Our strategy will be to demonstrate the descriptive power of an otherwise highly constrained phonological theory which incorporates the level of the CV-tier. We hope to show that, given this level, all of the phonological generalizations motivating the recognition of the syllable can be readily captured without the need for further notational apparatus.

Chapter 2: A Three-Tiered Theory of the Syllable

A universal theory of the syllable has, in our view, three specific tasks. First, it must specify the well-formed expressions of the theory. Thus, it provides an alphabet out of which syllable units are constructed together with a characterization of the permissable arrays of alphabetic units. Second, it must specify the parameters along which individual languages vary in their choice of syllable types. Third, it must characterize the class of language-particular rules which modify or extend the underlying syllable representations ("syllabification rules") and state how these rules are integrated into the general organization of the phonological component. We discuss each of these in turn in the following sections.

2.1 Well-formed Expressions

Let us consider, then, the first task. As we saw in Chapter 1, syllable trees consist of three-tiered representations, in which each tier has a certain vocabulary associated with it. The vocabulary of the first, or σ-tier, consists of the single element σ. The vocabulary of the second, or CV-tier, consists of the two elements C,V; and the vocabulary of the third, or segmental tier, consists of single-column phonetic matrices characterizing consonants and vowels in the usual manner. Well-formed strings on each tier consist of concatenations of the members of the alphabet defined on that tier.

Elements of neighboring tiers may be related in much the same way that syntactic elements are related in tree structures. In syntactic theory these relations are specified in terms of lines which are called "branches" while in multi-tiered phonological representations they are specified in terms of "association lines". The notion of "immediate constituent" holds in multi-tiered phonological representations just as it does in syntactic theory. Consider, for example, a tree of the following form:

Figure 1

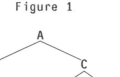

In structures like that in (1), B and C are said to be the immediate constituents of A because A immediately dominates each member of the string BC and nothing else.   Similarly, D and E are the immediate constituents of C. Furthermore, if a node A exhaustively dominates a string S and nothing else, S is said to be a member of the category A. Thus, the consonant /n/ and the sequence /dʒ/ in (5) of Chapter 1 are both members of the category C and the string /nɪf/ is a member of the category <u>syllable</u>.

While the similarity between syntactic trees and syllable trees is instructive, there are several differences which should be kept in mind. First, the notion of tier plays no significant   role in current syntactic theory. Thus, in the tiered representations presented here, the number of levels between the root and the terminals of a given structure is fixed at three. In syntactic trees no such fixed number is characterized.   Second, while in syllable theory the elements of the alphabet are exhaustively partitioned among the three tiers of syllable representation (i.e. each tier has its own alphabet and shares it with no other tier), in syntactic theory the non-terminal symbols may appear at any non-terminal level of the tree. A third difference concerns the nature of the inter-tier associations. In phrase structure trees, any non-root node must be immediately dominated by one and only one node. In multi-tiered phonological representations, however, non-root nodes may be dominated by two or more elements.

2.2 Core Syllables

We now turn to the second task of syllable theory, which involves the characterization of the set of syllable types encountered at the earliest level of phonological derivations. It is our view that words are fully syllabified at the level of lexical representation: that is, syllable trees are not built up in the course of phonological derivations but are already present, fully formed, in the lexical representations that constitute the input to the phonological component.[1] This is the strongest possible claim we can make with respect to syllable representation since it suggests that syllable structure is assigned at a single level, uniquely specifiable for all languages. A theory in which this is true is also the simplest possible theory from the point of view of acquisition since it entails that the syllable structures encountered in surface representation will be similar or identical to those found in underlying representation.

There are two types of evidence in favor of this view. First, there are languages in which the postulation of syllable structure in the lexicon makes it possible to achieve a significant simplification of the phonological component. Efik, which we discuss in greater detail below, is one such language. A second form of evidence is psycholinguistic in character and involves lexical recall tasks. For example, the so-called tip-of-the-tongue phenomenon reported on by Brown and McNeill (1966) and subsequent writers can be best understood in terms of a lexical entry that is fully syllabified. The tip-of-the-tongue phenomenon arises when subjects recall suprasegmental properties of a given lexical item such as stress placement and the number of syllables, but cannot recall properties characteristic of the segmental level of representation. Since these suprasegmental properties presuppose syllabification, such data suggests that words are

---

1. We return in Section 2.4 to a discussion of the algorithm whereby syllable structure is supplied to lexical representations.

stored in fully syllabified form.

We propose that the primary set of core syllable types comprises the following sequences:[2]

Figure 2

    a.   CV
    b.   V
    c.   CVC
    d.   VC

These syllable types are not equal in status, however. Notice first that all languages (to the best of our knowledge) have the syllable type CV, while some languages lack each of the other three types. Furthermore, type (2d) is the most highly marked in the sense that any language that has (2d) must also have (2a-c). It is possible to derive these systematic relationships in the following way. We propose that the syllable type CV belongs to the grammar of all languages. This syllable type may be operated on to yield one or more of the other core syllable types by the following two operations:

Figure 3

    a.   delete syllable initial C.
    b.   insert syllable final C.

Any language may choose either, both, or neither of these two rules to expand its inventory of primary core syllable types. This system thus gives rise to the following types of languages:

---

2. Proposals similar in spirit to those presented below are set out in Abercrombie (1967).

Figure 4

```
Type I:        CV
Type II:       CV, V
Type III:      CV, CVC
Type IV:       CV, V, CVC, VC
```

Type I involves neither rule in (3). Type II involves Rule (3a) alone. Type III involves Rule (3b) alone. Type IV involves both (3a) and (3b). Notice, in particular, that the following hypothetical language types cannot be characterized by the rules of (3):

Figure 5

```
V,   VC                        CV, V, CVC
CVC, VC                        CV, VC
CV, V, VC                      V, CVC
CV, CVC, VC                    V, VC, CVC
```

As far as we have been able to determine, each of the language types in (4) have been instantiated. For example, Type I is represented by Senufo, Type II by Maori, Type III by Klamath and Type IV by English. On the other hand, none of the types in (5) are instantiated.[3]

In addition to the parameters given in (3), languages may select among certain further options. First, some languages allow core syllable types to include sequences of consecutive V-elements:

---

3. This prediction of our theory clarifies and generalizes a claim made by Jakobson: "There are languages lacking syllables with initial vowels and/or syllables with final consonants, but there are no languages devoid of syllables with initial consonants or of syllables with final vowels." (Jakobson 1962, 526).

Figure 6

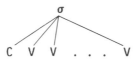

In such languages well-formed core syllable types may consist not only of CV and CVC, for example, but also of CVV and CVVC, and perhaps of CVVV and CVVVC and so on. Accordingly, we allow languages to freely select CV* as the representative of the primary core syllable (where V* represents one or more V-elements). If a language selects CV*, the operations of (3) apply as before to yield a set of derived core syllable types like those of (4) except for the fact that V* everywhere replaces V.

Similarly, some languages allow more than one C-element in initial or final position in the syllable. We represent this condition by C*. In order to expand our inventory of core syllable types to allow for the possibility of C* and V*, then, we will additionally define each language in terms of its maximal syllable, stated as a single expansion of the general schema $C(*)V(*)(C(*))$, where any occurrence of * may be replaced by an integer greater than 1. Thus, for example, the formula $C*V^2$ designates a language allowing syllable-initial clusters of any length and up to two vowels. The formula CV^2C^2 characterizes a language allowing two member consonant clusters in final position, but not in initial position in the syllable, and two member vowel clusters in the nucleus.   Using this notation, we may characterize the English core syllable in terms of the maximal syllable $C*VC^2$, realized fully by the English word sprint.[4] The symbol C* will be used in place of the more specific C^2, C^3, etc. when the upper bounds on the length of a cluster follow from language specific constraints on

---

4. We assume, following arguments presented in Kiparsky (1981), that longer syllables may be created by a rule adjoining extrasyllabic coronal segments to the end of a preceding syllable to form such words as next and sixth.

sequences of vowels and consonants within the syllable, and need not be independently stipulated.

Constraints on cooccurrence within the syllable are represented, in the present theory, by <u>positive</u> and <u>negative</u> syllable structure conditions which, taken together, generate the set of well-formed core syllables for each language. The positive syllable structure conditions (PSSCs) state the general canonic form of well-formed consonant or vowel clusters in terms of sequences of natural classes. For example, the PSSC in (8a) states that initial clusters may contain, as their first two (or only) members, any obstruent followed by any oral sonorant:

Figure 7

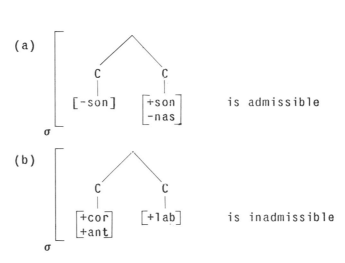

In case there are no constraints on clusters (a situation unknown to us in the case of consonant clusters, but not uncommon in the case of vowel sequences), no PSSC need be stated. The negative syllable structure conditions (NSSCs), applying to the output of the PSSCs, specify certain subsequences within the syllable as ill-formed, thus performing a filtering operation. For example, the NSSC (7b) excludes such sequences as /tw, dw, sw, zw/ from the set of consonant clusters generated by PSSC (7a). NSSCs range not only over subsequences dominated by Cs alone and subsequences dominated by Vs alone, but also subsequences dominated by both C and V elements. The empirical justification for the distinction between PSSCs and NSSCs will become apparent in our discussion of syllable initial clusters in English, in Section 2.5.

2.3 Core Syllable Associations

Permissible core syllable associations between elements of the CV-tier and elements of the segmental tier are determined in part by universal principles. Unless otherwise stipulated in the grammar or lexicon of a given language, V-elements of syllable structure are freely allowed to dominate [-consonantal] segments, and C-elements are freely allowed to dominate both [+ consonantal] segments and [+ high, -consonantal] segments. Other associations are possible only when admitted by language specific rules. For example, some languages allow post-vocalic consonants to be dominated by V if they are tautosyllabic with the preceding vowel. Languages of this type are those in which the "mora" is a unit of prosodic organization capable of bearing pitch or tone contrasts, and include Lithuanian, Japanese and Akan. As a further example, some languages allow tautosyllabic VC sequences to dominate single consonant or vowel segments. English is such a language in our view, since it has core syllables of the following type:

Figure 8

a.   σ   b.   σ

C V C C   C V C C

b   i   d   b   r   d

(8a) gives the underlying representation for the word <u>bide</u> which acquires its surface quality through the operation of rules of vowel shift and diphthongization. In core syllable representation, the vowel of this word is represented as a single segment assigned to two adjacent positions on the CV-tier, indicating that the vowel is long.   (8b), giving the underlying representation of <u>bird</u>, reflects the phonetic fact that the syllabic nucleus of this word does not contain a vowel such as we find in similar words like <u>breed</u> and <u>beard</u>. Rather, the portion of the utterance which occurs between the initial and final consonant presents a steady-state, r-colored segment occupying the syllable peak and consisting of two units of timing.[5] Accordingly, we represent this element as a single phonetic matrix associated with two elements of the CV-tier.

As we observed in Chapter 1, the "bipositional" representation of long vowels and consonants given in (8) allows us to formulate a unitary characterization of syllable weight.   Further motivation for such "bipositional" representation in English comes from an observation due to Selkirk (1978) regarding constraints on syllable final clusters. In the first place, Selkirk notes that in syllable final clusters of the form VCCC, where the vowel is short, the final member must be [+ coronal]. Thus, while <u>next</u> /nekst/ and <u>glimpse</u> /glɪmps/ are well-formed, words like like *<u>nexp</u> /neksp/ and *<u>glimpf</u> /glɪmpf/ are not. In the case of $\bar{V}$CC clusters, where the $\bar{V}$ is a long vowel or diphthong, the final consonant is subject to the same constraint; namely, it must be [+ coronal]. Thus, we find <u>pint</u> /paynt/ and <u>fiend</u> /fiynd/ but not /paynk/ or /fiymp/. It is clear that long vowels and diphthongs are functioning equivalently to VC sequences. If we express this equivalence by representing long vowels and diphthongs as suggested in (8), we may formulate a single constraint to the effect that the third member of a syllable final C cluster must dominate [+ coronal] segments

---

5. Cf. Klatt (1975) for measurements showing that stressed and unstressed syllabic /r/ in English have twice the length of stressed and unstressed non-low lax vowels, respectively, for one speaker.

only.[6]

In core syllable representations not all associations are one-to-one. We have just given examples of many-to-one associations in Figure (8) above. Additional one-to-many and many-to-one configurations are illustrated below:

Figure 9

As remarked earlier, the elements of the CV-tier are interpreted as corresponding to the <u>timing units</u> of speech production at the sub-syllabic level. Thus, a single C represents a single unit of timing, while a sequence CC represents a double timing unit. Accordingly, (9a) is interpreted as an affricate (i.e. a single, internally complex segment as in English <u>church</u>). We now have a natural way of distinguishing such minimal pairs as Polish <u>czy</u> 'whether' and <u>trzy</u> 'three', in which the affricate [tʃ] of the first example is acoustically and perceptually distinct from the otherwise identical stop-fricative sequence [tʃ] of the second (Brooks 1965):

---

6. In terms of the analysis suggested in footnote 4, in which the maximal core syllable of English is C*VC^2, this amounts to the requirement that extrasyllabic C elements are adjoined to the preceding syllable only if they dominate [+ coronal] segments.

Figure 10

'whether'   'three'

(9b) represents a geminate continuant such as is found in the core syllables of some languages. In English, geminate consonants are found in derived syllable structure in the casual pronunciation of phrases such as <u>of</u> <u>cour[ss]ey do</u> (i.e. <u>of course they do</u>). (See Shockey 1977 for further discussion.)

The availability of syllabifications involving many-one relationships provides a ready account for certain consonantal distributions which are otherwise puzzling. Consider, for example, the account of Efik given in Welmers (1973, 74-6). Welmers notes that this language has three sets of consonants which are differentiated by their distribution. Set 1 appears in both word-initial and intervocalic position; set 2 appears only in word-final position; and set 3 appears only intervocalically. Set 1, for example, is represented by the consonant [kp], set 2 by the consonant [p], and set 3 by the bilabial flap [B]. Thus we find, in word-initial position, examples like <u>kpók</u> 'cut up' (set 1); in word final position examples like <u>dép</u> 'buy' (set 2); but in intervocalic position examples from both sets 1 and 3, such as <u>èkpàt</u> 'bag' (set 1) and <u>sɨBé</u> 'cut down' (set 3).

Welmers notes that the consonants [kp] and [p] are in complementary distribution. Since Efik has the voiced phonemes /b/ and /d/ beside the voiceless phoneme /t/, he suggests, on grounds of pattern congruity, that [kp] is reasonably interpreted as representing a basic labial phoneme /p/ characterized by velar coarticulation. A phonetic rule removes the velar articulation in syllable-final position, thereby accounting for the final sound of <u>dep</u>.

But what of the bilabial flap [B]? Welmers notes that this flap is in complementary distribution with both [kp] and [p]. In particular, while it occurs intervocalically like [kp], it occurs only after vowels whose quality is elsewhere characteristic of vowels in closed syllables. To further illustrate this complementary distribution, Welmers provides the example <u>dwòp è bà</u> 'twelve (ten plus two)' which varies with the fast speech form <u>dwòBè bà,</u> where the closed syllable allophone of /o/ occurs in both cases.

In order not to proliferate the vocalic register of Efik, Welmers proposes, instead, to recognize the syllable as an entity in phonological description.[7] He then proposes that the flapped consonants that follow vowels showing closed syllable variants in words like <u>sɨBé</u>   are, in   fact, underlyingly ambisyllabic, as in (11a). Furthermore, Welmers proposes that the syllable structure of <u>dwòBè bà</u> in rapid speech be represented as in (11b), where the dashed line indicates the effect of a rule affiliating a word-final consonant to a vowel-initial syllable:

Figure 11

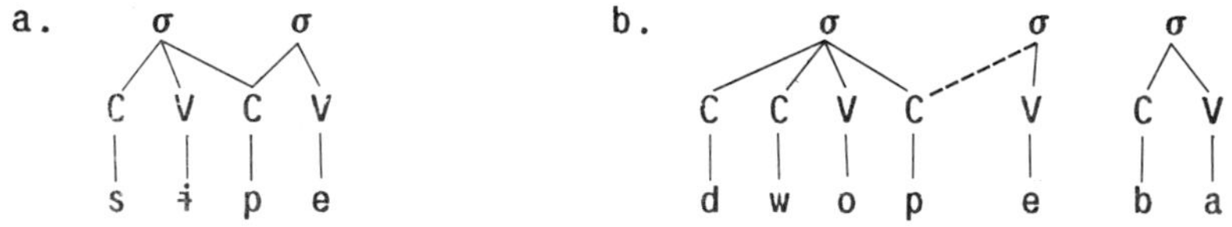

In these representations the ambisyllabic character of the medial /p/ is indicated by the fact that it is dominated by two syllable nodes. This /p/ undergoes the flap rule that applies to all ambisyllabic consonants, becoming [B].

7. In particular, he posits a unit to mark syllable division, although he does not make clear precisely how this unit is to be formally introduced. In what follows we adopt Welmers' basic insight but reformulate his analysis in terms of tree structures.

There are two consequences of Welmers' solution which argue overwhelmingly in its favor. First, the ambisyllabic representation of the medial /p/ causes the preceding syllable to be closed and thereby provides the requisite syllabic environment for the allophonic variation observed in the vowel system. Without this, it would be necessary, as Welmers notes, to virtually double the vowel inventory of Efik. Secondly, the representations in (11) provide the requisite syllabic environment to account for the allophonic variation observed between [kp], [p] and [B], assuming that the flap rule applies only to ambisyllabic consonants. Hence, the consonantal segments need not proliferate in the inventory of Efik phonemes.

2.4 Core Syllable Division

Elements of the CV-tier are grouped into core syllables corresponding to the core syllable inventory selected by the language in question. This grouping is constrained by the following principle:

Figure 12

The Onset First Principle

a. Syllable-initial consonants are maximized to the extent consistent with the syllable structure conditions of the language in question.

b. Subsequently, syllable-final consonants are maximized to the extent consistent with the syllable structure conditions of the language in question.

These two principles, which are adapted from rules formulated for English by Kahn (1976), apply in the order given. Hence, given a string of the form VCV, where both VC and CV are well-formed syllables, the syllable division is V-CV. Similarly, given a string of the form VCCV, where CCV is a well-formed syllable, the syllable division is V-CCV, even though VC (or VCC) may be well-formed syllables as well. Thus, the Onset First Principle implies that given alternative syllable divisions, languages will select that which maximizes syllable-initial consonant sequences.

Principle (12) might be interpreted in any number of empirically equivalent ways; for example, as conditions holding of fully formed core syllable representations, or of partly formed core representations which are then built up with reference to the language-particular syllable structure conditions to create fully formed core syllables. We adopt the latter interpretation here. In particular, we assume that fully formed core syllables are constructed in the following manner.

Figure 13

a. V-elements are prelinked to σ's.

b. C-elements to the left are adjoined one by one as long as the configuration resulting at each step satisfies all relevant syllable structure conditions.

c. Subsequently, C-elements to the right are adjoined in the manner described in (b) above.

To illustrate this algorithm, which builds up syllables in onionlike fashion from the center outward, we offer the following example:

Figure 14

a.

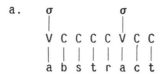

b.

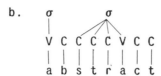

c.

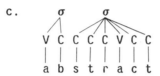

(14a) represents the initial configuration as defined by (13a). (14b) conflates three steps in accordance with (13b). The first of these creates the syllable /ra/, the second the syllable /tra/, and the third the syllable /stra/. As we see in Section 2.5, each of these intermediate configurations satisfies the syllable structure conditions of English pertaining to initial clusters. /b/ cannot be adjoined to the resulting configuration, however, since the sequence /bstr/ does not satisfy the conditions on syllable-initial position in English. The final configuration (14c) is then created in a similar manner in accordance with (13c).

According to the principles given so far, long clusters of consonants may not be exhaustively parsable into core syllables in some cases. Thus, some consonants in such clusters may remain extrasyllabic. An extrasyllabic consonant is one which is not a member of any syllable. Typically, such consonants are separated from neighboring consonants by short neutral or voiceless vowels and are historically susceptible to processes which either eliminate them or incorporate them into well-formed syllables by means of processes such as vowel epenthesis, sonorant vocalization and metathesis. English has several such examples. The usual pronunciation of knish in Cambridge, Massachusetts, for example, inserts a short, voiceless schwa after the k. However, this is not a full schwa as is evidenced by its near-minimal contrast with the word canoe. Other examples of extrasyllabic consonants in English include the initial consonants of the names Pnin, Knievel, Zbigniew, Khmer Rouge, Dvořák, Phnom Penh, Dmitri and Gdansk, in usual pronunciations, not to speak of the b in common renderings of the name of the former Iranian minister Ghotbzadeh. We represent extrasyllabic consonants as follows:

Figure 15

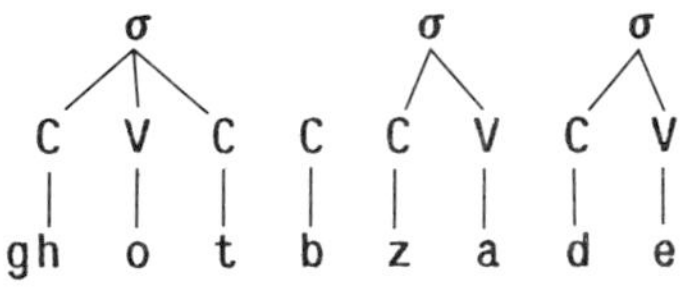

We claim that the segment b in an example such as this is a member of neither the first nor the second syllable, either underlyingly or on the surface. Extrasyllabic segments occurring in core syllable representations often play an important role in the syllable-conditioned phonology of languages. We return to this topic in Chapters 3 and 4.[8]

---

8. While our theory allows extrasyllabic C-elements, it does not permit extrasyllabic V-elements. This restriction follows from the logic of our theory. Given, first, that elements dominated by V are interpreted as belonging to the syllable peak, and second, that the notion of syllable peak is interpretable only with respect to a syllable of which the peak is a constituent, it follows that any notion of "extrasyllabic peak" would be conceptually anomalous.

2.5 A Case Study: Initial Consonant Clusters in English

We illustrate and develop the theory presented so far with a partial account of the core syllable in English. Here we consider the constraints on syllable-initial consonant sequences.

In terms of the set of parameters presented in Section 2.2, English is a Type IV language which permits consonant clusters (C*) in syllable-initial (and syllable-final) position. Specifically, as noted above, English conforms to the maximal syllable formula C^*VC^2. Initial consonant clusters are subject to a number of constraints. In the following figure we display in columnar format the well-formed and ill-formed initial clusters of English core syllable representations. The rows specify the first members of such clusters and the columns specify the second members. A " + " indicates that the row/column pair is a well-formed syllable-initial cluster, while a "-" indicates that it is not:

Figure 16

		w	l	r	p	t	k	m	n	f	θ
a.	p	-	+	+	-	-	-	-	-	-	-
	b	-	+	+	-	-	-	-	-	-	-
	f	-	+	+	-	-	-	-	-	-	-
b.	t	+	-	+	-	-	-	-	-	-	-
	d	+	-	+	-	-	-	-	-	-	-
	θ	+	-	+	-	-	-	-	-	-	-
c.	k	+	+	+	-	-	-	-	-	-	-
	g	+	+	+	-	-	-	-	-	-	-
d.	s	+	+	-	+	+	+	+	+	?	-
	ʃ	+	+	+	?	?	-	?	?	-	-

The following consonants do not occur as the first member of a cluster: /w, l, r, y, h, ð, z, ʒ, tʃ, dʒ, n, m, v/.

It will be noticed that no clusters containing /y/ have been included in the above chart. Following the analysis given by Levin (1981), we assume that /y/ in words such as <u>pure</u> or <u>cue</u> is not present underlyingly but is inserted by rule before the vowel /ɨ/, which becomes the surface /uw/.[9] This analysis receives support from two independent considerations. First, except for a few words of foreign orgin (for example, proper names such as <u>Tokyo</u>), /y/ appears in clusters before no other vowels than /uw/. This anomaly is explained under Levin's proposal by the fact that Cy clusters have no other source than the insertion rule. Secondly, /v/ and /m/, which do not otherwise appear in word-initial clusters in English, appear before /y/ in such words as <u>muse</u> and <u>view</u>. Under Levin's analysis, this /y/ is not underlying and thus these words do not constitute exceptions to the generalization that voiced fricatives and nasals do not occur as the first members of syllable-initial clusters in core syllable representations.

Let us examine more closely the cooccurrence restrictions given in (16). If we exclude for the moment the clusters of (16d), we observe that only obstruents occur as the initial member of these clusters, and only oral sonorants occur as the second member. On the basis of these observations we may formulate a <u>positive syllable structure condition</u> for two-member syllable-initial clusters as follows:

Figure 17

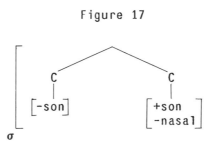

---

9. The rule of y-insertion does not apply in words like <u>poor</u> since there is no /ɨ/ at any point in their representation.

This condition is, needless to say, specific to English since many languages allow initial clusters that do not conform to it. It therefore forms a part of the set of rules constituting the phonological component of English.

(17) will correctly generate not only the clusters of (16a-c) but also the clusters in the first three columns of (16d). On the other hand, (17) is overly general in that it admits a number of clusters that are systematically excluded in English, as indicated by the minus entries in the table. Further examination shows that the exclusions are not random but fall into phonologically well-defined classes: labials may not be followed by /w/; nonstrident coronals are not followed by /l/; voiced fricatives are everywhere excluded as the first member of clusters; the sequence /sr/ is excluded; and finally, the second member of a cluster cannot be /y/. These observations motivate the following set of <u>negative syllable structure conditions</u> for English syllable-initial clusters: [10]

---

10. It should be noted that, following a suggestion by Halle and Vergnaud (1979), (18d) below can be eliminated in favor of a rule of the following sort: s → ʃ / __ r

Figure 18 - Negative Syllable Structure Conditions

condition: excludes:

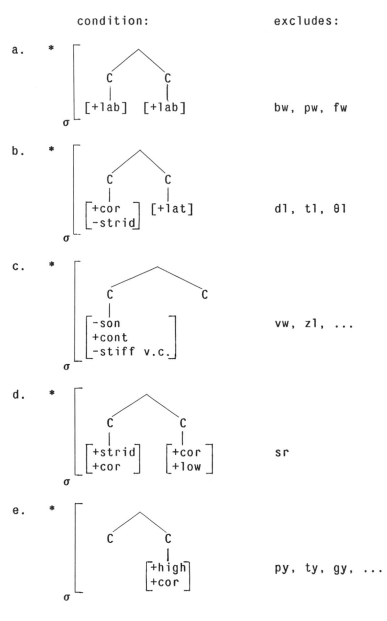

a.   *

C   C
| |
[+lab] [+lab]   bw, pw, fw
σ

b.   *

C   C
| |
⎡+cor ⎤ [+lat]   dl, tl, θl
⎣-strid⎦
σ

c.   *

C   C
|
⎡-son   ⎤   vw, zl, ...
⎢+cont   ⎥
⎣-stiff v.c.⎦
σ

d.   *

C   C
| |
⎡+strid⎤ ⎡+cor⎤   sr
⎣+cor ⎦ ⎣+low⎦
σ

e.   *

C   C
|
⎡+high⎤   py, ty, gy, ...
⎣+cor ⎦
σ

Let us now consider how the remaining s-initial clusters of (16d) are to be accounted for. Excluding for the moment the marginal cluster /sf/, which occurs only in a few items of the learned vocabulary, we find two further groups of s-clusters: /sp, st, sk/ and /sm, sn/. It should be clear that there is no obvious way to extend the positive syllable structure condition given in (17) to accommodate these clusters that does not involve the use of rather powerful notational devices permitting the expression of discontinuous dependencies.

As a first hypothesis, we might propose to account for these clusters in terms of the following additional positive conditions:

Figure 19

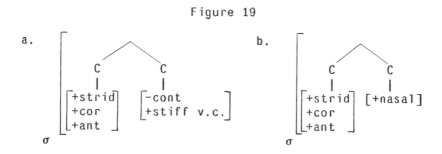

The first of these conditions admits /sp, st, sk/ while the second admits /sm, sn/. Notice, however, that these two conditions are partly similar, a fact which raises the question whether they may be simplified further. It appears that it is unnecessary to qualify condition (19a) by the feature [+ stiff v.c.]. Consider alternations such as the following:

Figure 20

```
believe / disbelieve
direct / misdirect
governor / ex-governor
hardball / softball
hug David / kiss David
lime green / grass green
```

In the first member of each pair, the initial stop of believe, direct, governor, ball, David and green can be pronounced with voicing throughout the articulation. The corresponding stop in the second member of each pair, however, is obligatorily devoiced (Davidsen-Nielsen 1974), except in the case of overly precise pronunciations in which a pause is inserted between the two constituents. This rule of devoicing, which devoices an oral stop after an unvoiced sound both within the same word and across word boundaries, is fully general and productive in English, and independently accounts for the absence of [sb, sd, sg], on the assumption that this rule is a non-cyclic rule in the sense of Mascaró (1976). There is, therefore, no need to incorporate this restriction in the set of syllable structure conditions. We may, accordingly, remove the specification [+stiff v.c.] from (19a). Observing now that /p, t, k, m, n/ all share the feature [-continuant], we may collapse the two statements of (19) into the following:

Figure 21 - Positive Syllable Structure Condition
(s-clusters)

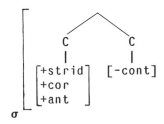

Turning now to three-member syllable-initial clusters, the important observation is that all such clusters are made up of overlapping sub-sequences of well-formed two-member clusters. The following three-member clusters are attested. [11]

Figure 22 - Three-member Syllable-initial Clusters

	w	l	r
sp	-	+	+
st	-	-	+
sk	+	+	+

Thus, for example, /spl/ is made up of the (overlapping) well-formed syllable-initial sequences /sp/ + /pl/. All sequences of three consonants that <u>cannot</u> be so parsed are excluded in English. Accordingly, /snr/ is not a possible three-member cluster, since /nr/ is not a possible two-member cluster.

It should be clear at this point that the set of occurring three-member clusters (and only these) is generated by the rules and principles given so far. Any three-member cluster, A B C, is analyzable into two two-member clusters, A B and B C, each of which necessarily satisfies either (17) or (21) and neither of which satisfies any of the negative syllable structure conditions (18). No other three-member clusters can be created under the algorithm stated in (13).

---

11. The cluster /skl/ is marginal, occurring in the learned vocabulary only: <u>sclerosis</u>, <u>sclaff</u>, <u>sklent</u> and in certain proper names such as <u>Sklar</u>. We consider its marginality accidental rather than systematic, although our decision here has no incidence upon the rest of our analysis.

Notice further, however, that while all well-formed three-member clusters can be analyzed into pairs of well-formed two-member clusters, it is not necessarily the case that any pair of well-formed two-member clusters, AB and BC, combine to form a well-formed three-member cluster, ABC. This is because of the requirement in the algorithm (13) that not only positive but also negative syllable structure conditions be satisfied. Thus, while both /st/ and /tw/ are well-formed two-member clusters in English, they cannot combine into a well-formed three-member cluster /stw/ because that cluster is ruled out by a negative syllable structure condition specific to this sequence.[12]

This system also makes the prediction that syllable-initial clusters in English consist of no more than three members. To see this, consider any arbitrary string of four consonants, ABCD. If consonants A and B satisfy condition (17), B and C satisfy neither (17) nor (21). Hence the string cannot be syllabified. Suppose, on the other hand, A and B satisfy condition (21). In this case consonants B and C can only satisfy condition (17). C and D, now, can satisfy neither condition (17) nor (21) and the string cannot be syllabified. Thus, it is an automatic consequence of our analysis that English contains initial clusters that are at most three segments long. This requires no independent statement in the grammar of English.[13]

To complete our analysis of initial consonant clusters in English core syllables, we consider first the observation that a few English words begin with /sf/ clusters. These include sphere, sphynx, sphragistics and a few proper names of foreign origin such as Svedberg, Sforza and Sfravara. This is most simply stated as a separate positive condition permitting the voiceless labial fricative /f/ after /s/;   /sfr/ clusters will then be automatically generated due to the independent acceptability of /fr/

---

12. In Clements and Keyser (1981) use was made of a Parsing Convention to account for the relation between two and three-member clusters in English. The present account eliminates the need for this convention.

13. We are indebted to Wendy Lewis for pointing out this consequence of our analysis to us.

clusters in core syllable representations. Secondly, the analysis so far does not accommodate certain /ʃ/-initial clusters which are fully integrated into the phonological systems of many monolingual English speakers, not only in words such as schwa, shrub and Schlesinger (as is predicted by (17)), but also in s[h]piel, shtick, schmalz and schnapps, which our analysis does not so far generate. The latter group of clusters may be admitted by a minimal generalization of (21) eliminating the feature [+ anterior]. Note that this generalization predicts the presence of three-member /ʃ/-initial clusters. The apparent absence of such clusters is probably best to be regarded as accidental in view of the relatively small number of words beginning with /ʃ/-initial clusters in the first place.[14]

Summarizing our analysis of initial consonant clusters in English core syllables, we have postulated two positive syllable structure conditions (17) and (21) (as well as a third, not formalized, for /sf/ clusters) and five negative syllable structure conditions (18a-e). These conditions, taken together, define the set of systematically possible (or well-formed) underlying initial consonant clusters in English core syllables.

As a further consequence of our analysis, we can explain the dual status of affricates with respect to syllable structure constraints. The affricate /tʃ/ behaves as a single segment in its ability to begin a syllable on its own; if we had treated it as a phoneme sequence, /t + ʃ/, it would have violated the positive syllable structure conditions (17) and (21). On the other hand, this segment behaves as a cluster with respect to the fact that it may not adjoin to a following liquid or glide to form any of the sequences /tʃr, tʃl, tʃw/. This fact follows automatically from the principles stated so far. Thus, note that a representation such as the following satisfies neither of the positive syllable structure conditions (17) or (21):

---

14. These clusters may not be totally absent, as witnessed by those speakers who allow initial /ʃ/ in such words as spritz, strudel, Strauss or Springer.

Figure 23

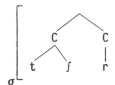

The representation of affricates as <u>single</u> segments on the CV-tier and as <u>dual</u> segments on the segmental tier enables us to account for their ambiguous status with respect to syllabification rules.

Our distinction between positive and negative conditions has been founded on the so far tacit premise that the language learner will learn the simplest set of conditions that characterizes the well-formed clusters of his or her language. This criterion is satisfied by the analysis given above. As the reader may verify, we cannot reformulate any of our existing positive conditions as negative conditions, or any of our negative conditions as positive conditions, without increasing the formal complexity of the analysis as determined by the usual evaluation metrics. In addition, our analysis has been carried out under the further assumption that syllable structure conditions are properly stated in terms of a highly restricted vocabulary which does not include the abbreviatory conventions or other notational devices that have been proposed elsewhere in phonology. Thus, while we could have collapsed our two positive conditions or any two or more of our negative conditions by the use of angled brackets subject to Boolean conditions, we have not done so due to our belief that such abbreviations do not reflect genuine linguistic generalizations concerning core syllable structure.

These methodological premises lead us to an interesting empirical consequence. Our analysis has recognized two classes of "systematically excluded" clusters: those that are not generated by the positive conditions, and those that are excluded by the negative conditions. These two classes of clusters are of a strikingly different character. The clusters not generated by the positive conditions are totally deviant sequences. These include such sequences as /zb, bd, dv, bz/, which, as we have already seen in our discussion of extrasyllabicity, cannot be pronounced as tautosyllabic sequences by phonetically untrained English speakers. Further such sequences as /rb, wt, lr, nk/, etc., which are equally deviant, are also excluded by the positive conditions. Exceptions to our generalization, we believe, are only apparent. Thus, the initial sound of the name Nkrumah is pronounced as a separate syllable by most monolingual English speakers, while the initial sequences of words such as tsetse and tsar are probably to be considered as affricates (which are not, as we have seen, excluded by the syllable structure conditions). If we consider, on the other hand, the further class of "systematically excluded" syllables which is excluded by the negative syllable structure conditions, we find a very different state of affairs. These sequences, in large part, are not only easily pronounceable by the phonetically untrained speaker but occur with some frequency in words of foreign origin. Examples include fjord, Kyoto, bwana, pueblo, Tlingit, Vladimir, zweiback, vroom, voyeur, foie gras, svelte and so on. We believe that the traditional confusion regarding whether clusters such as these should be accounted for in a general account of the English syllable[15] reflects their intermediate status between fully acceptable and fully deviant clusters. This difference is formally characterized in the present approach by the fact that they are excluded by negative, rather than positive

---

15. See Algeo (1978) for a useful review of the literature.

conditions on syllable structure.[16]

2.5.1 Excursus: The Acquisition of Consonant Clusters

There are very few detailed longitudinal studies of the acquisition of phonology and only one, to our knowledge, which bears directly on the acquisition of syllable-initial clusters in English, that of Smith (1973). Smith found that the acquisition of initial clusters was characterized by a highly systematic progression of stages, each exhibiting fewer restrictions on consonant cooccurrence than the previous stage. Interestingly, three-member clusters were reported to appear at the same time as the two-member clusters of which they were constituted; thus, /spl/ appeared at the point when /pl/ was already present and /sp/ had just been acquired (p. 169).

This result is of theoretical interest for language acquisition. Consider, in particular, the view of acquisition expressed in Jakobson (1968). Jakobson observed that, all else being equal, syntagmatically simple sequences are acquired earlier than syntagmatically more complex ones. Specifically, Jakobson claimed that within a word, the maximum number of

---

16. In an earlier study Greenberg and Jenkins (1964) examined the linguistic distance of monosyllables from well-formed English along a four-point scale as follows:
   1. existing word: well-formed existing cluster - /strʌk/
   2. nonexisting word: well-formed existing cluster - /strib/
   3. nonexisting word: well-formed nonexisting cluster - /stwip/
   4. nonexisting word: ill-formed nonexisting cluster - /gvsurs/
An implication of their findings was that "...the perceptual sensitivity of the subjects to [linguistic distance from English] is uniform across the entire length of the scale as opposed to being highly sensitive for small departures from English and less and less sensitive for differences between very distant 'words'" (p. 167). Note that Greenberg and Jenkins did not test the validity of their four-point scale directly, but rather the validity of a scale of distance from English as measured by the number of ways we can perform phoneme substitutions in four-phoneme "words" and arrive at existing words (the more ways, the closer the word is to English).

Our results motivate the recognition of a subdivision in the fourth point of this scale; namely, a subdivision into ill-formed clusters that are excluded by negative conditions (pwin) and those that are excluded by positive conditions (pkin).

phonemes, the number of their possibilities of distribution, and the maximum number of phonemic distinctions all increase by degrees in child language acquisition (op.cit. pp.85-86). While this claim is probably correct as a broad and general one, it does not allow us to accommodate Smith's results in any straightforward way, since it would predict that /sp/ and /pl/ clusters would be acquired earlier than /spl/ clusters. On the assumption that a child's knowledge of English phonology includes knowledge of the positive syllable structure conditions (17) and (21), however, Smith's result is what we expect to find. Once a child has acquired two-member clusters like /sp/ and /pl/, this condition predicts that the child has concurrently acquired the competence to produce three-member clusters such as /spl/.

Due to the lack of relevant studies, we do not know whether all children show the same pattern of behavior as Smith's subject. In fact, we would not be surprised to find a lag in the production of three-member clusters in some subjects caused by performance difficulties due, perhaps, to differing rates of physical maturation. Until such time as more data is available, we can do no more than note that Smith's otherwise anomalous observation finds a natural explanation within our framework.

2.6 Syllable Transformations

Up to this point we have described how languages construct a core syllable inventory by selecting among the limited number of parameters provided by the theory. We have so far said nothing about the third task of syllable theory, that of characterizing the class of processes which transform core syllable representations into the frequently distinct set of surface syllable trees. It is obvious that such processes play an important role in the phonological systems of many languages; see, for example, the discussion of Klamath syllabification given in Chapters 4 and 5. Some of these processes affect elements of the segmental tier exclusively, while some affect higher levels of representation. We number among these operations the following: the insertion and deletion of association lines, and the insertion, deletion, substitution and metathesis of segments on the CV-tier.

Operations affecting syllable structure are governed by certain general conventions that apply automatically to their output. Their general effect is to preserve phonological well-formedness throughout derivations. Thus, phonological rules which apply so as to create ill-formed syllables will generally induce the operation of applicable well-formedness conditions. We shall not illustrate all of these conventions here as we shall have ample opportunity to do so in the discussion to follow. However, we shall pause to mention one particularly pervasive convention, that which deals with resyllabification.

In many languages we find that the constraints on syllable structure hold not only at the level of core syllable representation, but also after the application of phonological rules. We may express this fact by assuming that in such languages the rules of syllabification continue to apply throughout phonological derivations in accordance with the Resyllabification Convention given below:

Figure 24 - Resyllabification Convention

The output of every rule is resyllabified according to the syllable structure rules examined up to that point in the derivation.

We interpret this convention to mean that all association lines between C-elements and σ's, as well as all floating σ's, are erased, and that the resulting configuration is resyllabified according to the algorithm stated in (13).

Whenever, in the course of a derivation, resyllabification is called for, we assume that all syllabification rules encountered previously in that derivation will reapply. This includes not only those syllabification rules belonging to the core syllable component, but those belonging to the phonological component as well, and includes affiliation rules of the type to be examined just below and in Chapter 4. We add two further comments on the Resyllabification Convention. First, this convention may cease to operate late in derivations in some languages, where, for example, vowel elision may create consonant clusters, extrasyllabic segments or other such sequences that are ill-formed in earlier stages of derivation. We propose, then, that individual grammars may specify a point in the set of ordered rules at which the Resyllabification Convention becomes inoperative; indeed, some languages may not make use of the Resyllabification Convention at all. Second, there is evidence that in some languages at least, syllabification takes place initially at the domain of the morpheme and subsequently at the level of the stem or word. Resyllabification across word boundaries, on the other hand, is normally optional, and may differ in some respects from initial syllabification. For some discussion see Kiparsky (1979), Harris (1983) and Odden (forthcoming).

We turn finally to a class of rules which effect association lines by explicitly introducing, deleting or respecifying them. Such is the effect, for example, of the rule of "Right Capture" (Kahn 1976), which creates ambisyllabic segments in words such as <u>Monica</u>:

Figure 25

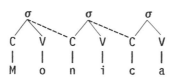

This rule, which affects intervocalic consonants in unstressed syllables, has the sole effect of introducing the association lines indicated by the dashed lines in (25). It accounts for the phonetic fact that the first and second syllables of <u>Monica</u> are closed and that the second and third consonants are ambisyllabic. We may assume, harmlessly, that the Resyllabification Convention (24) applies to the result of rules of this type just as it does to all others. Since it requires that the structure be resyllabified according to the syllable structure rules examined up to that point in the derivation (thus, including the affiliation rule illustrated in (25) itself), its effect is vacuous, and (25) remains unchanged. We refer the reader to Kahn (1976) for a fuller account of the role of affiliation rules in English, including rules not mentioned in the above discussion.[17]

---

17. The rules of English given in this chapter predict that /s/ is syllabified rightward in sequences of the form: VsC_1V. This syllabification seems correct for most examples. Kahn (1976) points out that the location of main stress in nouns such as <u>amnesty</u>, <u>orchestra</u> and <u>pedestal</u> indicates that the penultimate syllable is light, and hence that the /s/ initial cluster is tautosyllabic with the following vowel. Other examples, however, seem to suggest that /s/ clusters are heterosyllabic in some cases; for example, <u>asbestos</u>, <u>manifesto</u>, <u>clandestine</u> and <u>fiesta</u>, which receive penultimate stress. However, numerous further examples like <u>allegro</u>, <u>vanilla</u>, <u>regatta</u> and <u>Kentucky</u> exhibit penultimate stress even though their penultimate syllables are light. To attract penultimate stress to these syllables, we may provide these words with idiosyncratically marked closed syllables in the lexicon, or, alternatively, provide them with lexically marked stress. The same solution can then be extended to words like <u>asbestos</u>.

Chapter 3: Evidence for the Theory

In this chapter we review the evidence motivating the theory of the syllable presented in Chapter 2. We first examine evidence for the syllable tier, and we then examine evidence for the CV-tier. A final section examines syllabification processes in French.

3.1 Evidence for the Syllable Tier

In general, evidence establishing the need for recognizing such notions as "syllable," "syllable-initial (or syllable-final) position," "tautosyllabicity," "ambisyllabicity," and "extrasyllabicity" can be taken as evidence for formal recognition of the syllable as an entity in phonological representation. There have, of course, been a number of quite different proposals for representing the syllable within generative phonology, including the use of boundary symbols (Hooper 1972), improper bracketing (Anderson and Jones 1974) and indexing (Venneman 1979), in addition to the hierarchical mode of representation first proposed by Kahn and developed here. It would take us well beyond the scope of the present work to compare and evaluate the relative adequacy of these various alternatives. It is appropriate to point out, however, that each of the notions mentioned above receives a natural interpretation within the present formalism. Thus:

Figure 1

i. a string of segments S is a <u>syllable</u> iff there is a node σ such that σ dominates each member of S and nothing else (cf. Chapter 2.1).

ii. a segment P is in <u>syllable-initial</u> (<u>syllable-final</u>) position iff there is a node σ such that P is the leftmost (rightmost) segment dominated by σ. Furthermore, P is in <u>absolute</u> syllable-initial (syllable-final) position if P is not ambisyllabic.

iii. two segments P, Q are <u>tautosyllabic</u> iff they are dominated by the same node σ.

iv. a segment P is <u>ambisyllabic</u> iff it is dominated by two nodes σ.

v. a segment P is <u>extrasyllabic</u> iff it is dominated by no node σ.

A minimal condition of adequacy upon a theory of the syllable is that it should characterize all the notions of (1i-v). We take the need for notions (1i-iii) as having been amply justified in the phonological literature. Kahn (1976) has offered extensive, and to our minds convincing justification for the notion of ambisyllabicity (1iv).[1] We offer further evidence for the notion of ambisyllabicity in our discussion of Danish, below (see also the discussion of Efik in Chapter 2). The role of extrasyllabicity (1v) is discussed in Halle and Vergnaud's illuminating treatment of Harari and Berber (1979) and in Michelson's detailed study of Mohawk epenthesis (1981). We shall elaborate upon this notion briefly here.

The strongest language-internal evidence for the linguistic reality of the syllable comes from the fact that it allows us to eliminate arbitrariness in stating the phonological contexts in which the various syllable-sensitive rules of a given language apply. An example will make this point clear. Consider the following data from Turkish:

---

1. Kiparsky (1979) offers an alternative interpretation of the facts cited by Kahn within a framework making use of the independently-needed notion "foot". This framework neither requires, nor as far as we can see, precludes the characterization of ambisyllabic segments. Thus, in any given case, it is an empirical question, both within Kiparsky's theory and ours, whether given segments are to be characterized as ambisyllabic or not.

Figure 2

		Acc.	Nom.	Abl.
a.	Degemination:			
	'feeling'	hiss+i	his	his+ten
	'right'	hakk+ɨ	hak	hak+tan
	'price increase'	zamm+ɨ	zam	zam+dan
b.	Epenthesis:			
	'transfer'	devr+i	devir	devir+den
	'bosom'	koyn+u	koyun	koyun+dan
	'abdomen'	karn+ɨ	karɨn	karɨn+dan
c.	Vowel Shortening:			
	'time'	zama:n+ɨ	zaman	zaman+dan
	'warning'	i:ka:z+ɨ	i:kaz	i:kaz+dan
	'proof'	ispa:t+ɨ	ispat	ispat+tan
d.	Final Devoicing:			
	'ruined'	hara:b+ɨ	harap	harap+tan
	'Ahmed'	ahmed+i	ahmet	ahmet+ten
	'color'	reng+i	renk	renk+ten
e.	k-Deletion:			
	'cow'	ine+i	inek	inek+ten
	'logic'	mantɨ+ɨ	mantɨk	mantɨk+tan
	'foot'	aya+ɨ	ayak	ayak+tan

These alternations can be most simply explained if we assume that the underlying representation of the stems in (2a-d) is identical to the (surface) accusative stem, and the underlying representation of the stems in (2e) is identical to the (surface) nominative stem. The processes illustrated in (2) may then be described as follows. By Degemination, a geminate consonant is simplified word-finally and before a consonant-initial suffix. By Epenthesis, an epenthetic vowel is inserted between two consonants word-finally, and before a consonant-initial suffix. By Vowel Shortening, a long vowel becomes a short vowel before a consonant which is word-final or which precedes a consonant-initial suffix. By Final Devoicing, a voiced oral stop is devoiced word-finally, or before a consonant-initial suffix.   By k-Deletion, k̠ is deleted after a short vowel if another vowel follows immediately (i.e. provided the k̠ is not word-final or followed by a consonant-initial suffix).[2] This brief statement is sufficient to demonstrate that the configuration:

$$C \quad \left\{ \begin{array}{c} \# \\ C \end{array} \right\}$$

plays an important role in Turkish phonology.   The recurrence of this configuration is unexplained in a theory that does not recognize the syllable as a phonological entity.

In order to explain the forms in (2), then, we will assume that Turkish has a core syllable component that defines the notion "well-formed syllable" in that language.   The forms in (2) demonstrate that Turkish has syllables of all the following types: CV, V, CVC, VC.   Thus, Turkish may be identified as a Type IV language.   We further see that Turkish allows the V* option, but that long vowel syllables may not end with a consonant.   Short vowel syllables, as already noted in Chapter 1, may terminate with a single consonant or with two-member clusters of the following types: (a) sonorant plus obstruent, (b) fricative plus stop, or (c) /k/ plus /s/. Thus the maximal syllable in Turkish is CV^*C^2, subject to a NSSC precluding a C after VV.

Given these observations, together with the Onset First Principle (12), we see that the processes illustrated in (2a-c) have the single effect of eliminating extrasyllabic segments from representations, either by deleting them (Degemination), inserting an epenthetic vowel (Epenthesis), or else

---

2. This rule is triggered by a restricted class of suffixes as explained by Sezer (1981), to whom we are indebted for discussion of the facts summarized here.

deleting one mora of a long vowel (Vowel Shortening). These processes are illustrated below; note that automatic resyllabification takes place in the second and third examples:

Figure 3

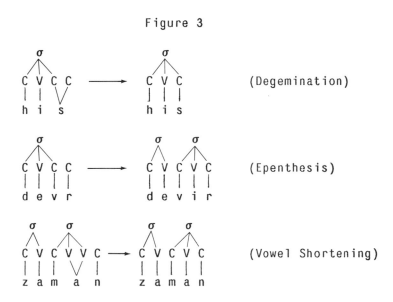

(Degemination)

(Epenthesis)

(Vowel Shortening)

By definition (1v), the final consonant in all these examples is extrasyllabic prior to the operation of the rules in question. The rules apply to create configurations which can be fully syllabified. Notice that there is no way of predicting the way these rules apply on the basis of universal principles of syllabification; the rules in question represent the particular means by which Turkish has responded to the configurational complexity created by extrasyllabic consonants. We conclude that phonological theory must recognize the existence of extrasyllabic segments if it is to provide an adequate account of syllable conditioned phonological processes.

We return to a discussion of extrasyllabicity in Chapter 4, where we discuss vowel epenthesis processes in Klamath.

3.2 Evidence for the CV-tier

We now turn to a consideration of the evidence for incorporating a CV-tier into a general theory of the syllable. To begin with, we shall state our general assumptions. We propose, following Clements (1978, 1982) and McCarthy (1981), that the relation beween the terminal and preterminal elements of syllable trees is analogous to the relation between adjacent tiers in other autosegmental systems such as tone and vowel harmony systems. In particular, this relationship is governed by the same set of conventions in all cases. Slightly different versions of these conventions are given in Clements and Ford (1979), Clements (1981) and McCarthy (1981). As we know of no evidence bearing upon the choice of these alternatives, which vary only slightly with regard to their empirical implications, we give the simplest version of them here in accordance with Clements (1981).

A minimal autosegmental representation consists of two tiers. Each of these tiers has assigned to it certain designated classes of features. One tier consists of a sequence of segments termed autosegments. The other consists of a sequence of segments which include what we term anchors; that is, designated classes of segments to which autosegments are linked under the Association Conventions to be stated below. An autosegment linked to an anchor will be termed the associate of that anchor and, conversely, an anchor linked to an autosegment will be termed the associate of that autosegment. We propose that the class of anchors in a given autosegmental system is partly determinable on universal grounds in terms of the following statements:

Figure 4

a. tonal autosegments are anchored to V-elements or σ-elements of syllable structure;

b. vowel harmony autosegments are anchored to vowels (i.e. nonconsonantal segments dominated by V);

c. <u>nonconsonants</u> are anchored to V-elements of syllable structure;

d. <u>consonants</u> are anchored to C-elements of syllable structure.

These statements define the classes of segments that are linked to each other under the universal Association Conventions. Further classes of segments may be linked to each other either lexically or by rule in individual languages. For example, in Zulu "depressor consonants" are associated with low tones by a rule of the phonology; see Laughren (in press) for discussion. Thus, the class of anchors defined in (4) designates the class of segments subject to the Association Conventions, not the larger class of segments that may be linked to autosegments by language specific rules or other principles.

We state the Association Conventions as follows:

Figure 5

a. Link free (unassociated) autosegments with free anchors pairwise from left to right until either no further autosegments or no further anchors remain:

b. Given a string of free anchors remaining after the operation of (5a), associate each anchor with the nearest available autosegment, giving precedence to the autosegment on the left.

anchors

autosegments

These conventions are principles of universal grammar, characterizing the "unmarked" pattern of association between autosegmental tiers, and apply automatically whenever they are defined in a phonological derivation.

Let us consider now a range of evidence demonstrating the empirical justification for the CV-tier.

3.3 Mapping

The first argument for the CV-tier that we shall cite here is drawn from McCarthy's extensive discussion of word formation processes in Classical Arabic (1981). A representative sample of stems constructed from the root ktb 'write' is given below:

Figure 6

Binyan	Perfective		Imperfective	
	Active	Passive	Active	Passive
I	katab	kutib	aktub	uktab
II	kattab	kuttib	ukattib	ukattab
III	kaatab	kuutib	ukaatib	ukaatab
IV	ʔaktab	ʔuktib	uʔaktib	uʔaktab

Each binyan represents a different derivational category. This small sample of forms is sufficient to suggest a number of generalizations. First, each form contains the discontinuous root sequence /k...t...b/. Second, each column is characterized by its own special vowel sequence. Thus the first column forms are characterized by the vowel a; the second column forms by the vowel sequence ui; the third column forms (discounting the first binyan form) by the vowel sequence uai; and the fourth column forms by the vowel sequence ua. A third generalization is that each binyan selects one among a small set of possible canonical syllable patterns. Thus, binyan I selects the (underlying) pattern CVCVC; binyan II selects the pattern CVCCVC; binyan III selects CVVCVC; and binyan IV selects CVCCVC.[3]

McCarthy has shown that the word formation processes in Classical Arabic illustrated in (6) can best be characterized if we recognize the CV-tier (in McCarthy's terminology, the prosodic template) as an independent element of phonological representation. In McCarthy's account, a word is minimally constructed from three morphemes: a sequence of consonants, a sequence of vowels, and a sequence of CV elements. Each is arrayed on a separate tier. Mapping proceeds according to the Association Conventions (5), supplemented by a small number of language particular rules. Under this account, for example, the word ktaabab (binyan XI, perfective active) is represented in underlying form as follows:

---

3. Two comments are in order. First, vowel sequences in the first binyan alternate in a complex set of ablaut patterns which deviate from the patterns regularly found elsewhere, explaining the apparently anomalous vowel sequence of aktub. Second, the imperfective forms are characterized by a prefixed CV sequence of which only the V-element is represented in (6); the identity of the prefixed consonant is determined by subject agreement. The apparently irregular canonic shape of the imperfective forms of the first binyan is determined by a rule which reduces underlying CVCVCVC patterns to CVCCVC patterns by elision of the medial V-element. These and other points are discussed at length in McCarthy (1981), where extensive justification is given for the analysis briefly summarized here.

Figure 7

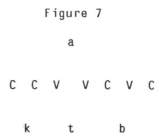

Application of convention (5a) yields the solid lines and application of (5b) the dashed lines in the following:

Figure 8

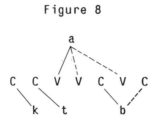

The recognition of the prosodic template as a separate tier of representation is motivated by the fact that its identity remains constant for different lexical roots as well as for different inflectional categories (aspect, as well as voice).

3.4 Unassociated CV Elements

A second type of argument for the CV-tier comes from languages which offer evidence of C-elements or V-elements which are unassociated with vowels and consonants in underlying representations. Such unassociated elements induce the automatic spreading of accessible consonants and vowels on the segmental tier. It can also be shown that they condition certain phonological rules.

3.4.1 Turkish

As a first example we return to Turkish.[4] Consider, to begin with, the suffix alternations illustrated in the following forms:

Figure 9

		nom.	nom. pl.	dat.	3sg.poss.	2pl. poss.
a.	room	oda	odalar	odaya	odasɨ	odanɨz
	river	dere	dereler	dereye	deresi	dereniz
	bee	arɨ	arɨlar	arɨya	arɨsɨ	ariniz
b.	cap	kep	kepler	kepe	kepi	kepiniz
	stalk	sap	saplar	sapa	sapɨ	sapɨnɨz
	Ahmed	ahmet	ahmetler	ahmede	ahmedi	ahmediniz

(9a) and (9b) represent the regular treatment of vowel-final and consonant-final stems, respectively. Here we shall abstract from the vowel quality alternations due to vowel harmony, and concentrate upon the number of segments in alternating suffixes. The suffixes of interest are therefore those of the final three columns. We see that after the vowel-final

---

4. We are again indebted to Engin Sezer for valuable discussion. For a historical perspective on the forms discussed below, see Sezer (1982).

stems of (9a), these three suffixes have the shape /-yE, -sI, -nIz/, respectively, while after the consonant-final stems of (9b), the same suffixes have the shape /-E, -I, -InIz/. (We use capital letters to represent vowels which alternate regularly under vowel harmony.) The underlying form of these suffixes must be assumed to be /-yE, -sI, -InIz/, respectively. The forms of (9) thus show that Turkish has rules of suffix allomorphy which, among other things, delete suffix-initial consonants after stem-final consonants and suffix-initial vowels after stem-final vowels.[5]

There is a set of stems ending in long vowels that does not conform to the above generalizations. Consider the following representative examples:

Figure 10

mountain	da:	da:lar	daa	daɨ	daɨnɨz
avalanche	cɨ:	cɨ:lar	cɨa	cɨɨ	cɨɨnɨz
dew	ci:	ci:ler	cie	cii	ciini

We see that the suffixes here show the same alternants that they showed after the consonant-final stems of (9b); in other words, these stems are treated phonologically as though they were consonant-final.[6] We could easily predict these alternants if we could postulate a final consonant in the underlying representations of the stems. However, such a consonant never appears on the surface. Moreover, no phonological rule of Turkish gives us any indication of what the identity of such an "abstract" consonant might be: the phonological rules of Turkish would operate equally well whether we take this hypothetical consonant to be /γ/, or /θ/, or /β/, for example. For this reason such an analysis seems undesirably arbitrary.

---

5. The class of suffixes which undergo these rules is partly arbitrary. See, for further examples, Lewis 1967.

6. Historically the nouns in question ended in the voiced velar fricative known as yumuşak ge (orthographically, ğ), which has been entirely lost in standard Turkish, although reflexes of these consonants survive as velar glides in some non-standard dialects.

On the other hand, it also seems inadequate simply to consider these forms as underlyingly vowel-final, and to mark them with a diacritic feature (say, [+X]). Such a feature is no less "abstract" than the hypothetical consonant of the alternative just considered, since it has no phonological manifestation. Moreover, while we could extend the rules we have motivated so far to account for these cases by allowing them to refer to the presence (or absence) of the feature [+X], such an analysis would fail to explain the fact that all the stems in this class behave uniformly as if they were consonant-final with regard to several formally independent rules of the grammar.

In short, neither the "abstract" nor the "concrete" approaches are fully satisfactory in accounting for the behavior of the stems in (10). A final proposal can be similarly eliminated: we cannot formulate the rules of suffix allomorphy in such a way as to class all long vowel stems together with consonant stems in opposition to short vowel stems, since there is a further class of long vowel stems that behave in parallel to the short vowel stems of (9); some examples follow:

Figure 11

la (musical note)	la:	la:lar	la:ya	la:si	la:nɨz
spelling	imla:	imla:lar	imla:ya	imla:sɨ	imla:nɨz
building	bina:	bina:lar	bina:ya	bina:si	bina:nɨz

Intuitively, we would like to be able to represent the forms in (10) as somehow having a final consonant in their underlying representation, without committing ourselves as to what, exactly, that final consonant might be. In the autosegmental framework developed here, this can be done quite simply by postulating a free C-element in these forms which does not dominate a phonetic feature matrix on the segmental tier. Thus, the long vowels in (10) will correspond to the sequence VC on the CV-tier, while those of (11) correspond to the sequence VV. Following this proposal, the underlying representations of 'mountain' and 'la' are as follows:

Figure 12

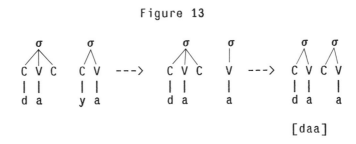

'mountain'   'la' (musical note)

The application of the rules of suffix allomorphy will be sensitive to whether the stem ends in a C or a V.   However, the identity of the specific consonants and vowels on the segmental tier is irrelevant to the operation of the rules under discussion; thus, stems ending in C-elements that dominate no segmental material will behave just the same as stems whose final C-elements dominate segmental material.   Returning to the example under discussion, then, since 'mountain' ends in a C-element, it triggers the rule deleting the initial consonant of the dative morpheme. The output of this rule then undergoes resyllabification (cf. (24), Chapter 2). The derivation proceeds as follows:

Figure 13

In cases where the free C-element cannot be resyllabified by the core syllable rules of Turkish, it undergoes a rule affiliating it to the preceding vowel. We formulate this rule as follows:

Figure 14

This rule accounts for the nominative singular and plural forms of (10) as follows:

Figure 15

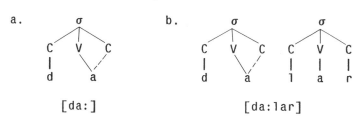

It can easily be seen that the present analysis does not incorporate the disadvantages of the "abstract" and "concrete" approaches considered earlier. First, it is a nonabstract solution in the sense that all elements postulated in underlying representation appear on the surface as well. Specifically, the free C-elements attributed to the stems of type (10) survive either as (unpronounced) onsets of syllables, as in the final three columns, or as the second mora of the long vowels, as in the remaining forms. Secondly, unlike the diacritic solution, it accounts for the uniform behavior of the stems of (10) with respect to the rules of suffix allomorphy: these stems behave "as if" they were consonant-final precisely because they are consonant-final in all respects relevant to the operation of the rules.

There are, moreover, two further advantages of the present analysis. First, it will be seen that the stem vowel in the forms of (10) alternates between long and short values, the short variants occurring before vowel-initial suffixes. These length alternations are automatically accounted for under the present analysis, as a glance at (13) and (15) will show. In (13), illustrating the dative form, the root vowel is short because the "empty" C-element is no longer tautosyllabic with it after resyllabification, and thus fails to trigger rule (14). Only in the nominative forms (15) (and other forms involving consonant-initial suffixes) is the environment of this rule met. Thus, the process of prevocalic vowel shortening is not a separate rule of Turkish grammar, but a concomitant effect of resyllabification.

A second advantage concerns a phonetic observation not yet commented on. It will be seen that both the dative and nominative forms of 'mountain' in (10) are transcribed as having long vowels, but with a difference: the long vowel of the dative is transcribed [aa], and that of the nominative [aː]. To this difference in transcription corresponds a difference in phonetics: the vowel of the dative is perceptibly longer than that of the nominative and involves a type of phonation sometimes termed "vowel rearticulation": a mode of production in which the vowel is uttered with two intensity peaks. These phonetic differences are consequences of the analysis given so far. The phonological representation assigned to the nominative characterizes this form as a monosyllable, with three units along the CV-tier (see (15a)), while the dative is represented as a bisyllabic form with four units along the CV-tier (see (13)). Given our assumption that units of the CV-tier represent timing units at the subsyllabic level, the relative length of the two forms is predicted, while the "rearticulation" of the long vowel of the dative follows from the fact that it forms the peak of two successive syllables.

In summary, then, Turkish offers strong support for the recognition of the CV-tier as a central level of prosodic organization in phonological representation. Furthermore, it presents crucial evidence for the distinction between C-elements and V-elements on this tier as it is this distinction that permits a straightforward account of the contrast between two phonologically distinct types of long vowels in this language.[7]

3.4.2 Finnish

Finnish offers a further and equally instructive case of unassociated C and V elements. There is a phonological process in Finnish known as gradation whereby a geminate consonant cluster is simplified if the second member of the geminate cluster occurs in the onset of a closed syllable. Examples of this phenomenon are given below:

Figure 16

	nom.	gen.	part.	iness.	adess.
'hat'	hattu	hatun	hattua	hatussa	hatulla
'priest'	pappi	papin	pappia	papissa	papilla
'cork'	korkki	korkin	korkkia	korkissa	korkilla

In these forms the endings are as follows: nominative = Ø, genitive = n, partitive = ta,[8] inessive = ssa, adessive = lla. These forms clearly indicate the relevant distributional fact; namely, a geminate consonant cluster is replaced by the corresponding non-geminate consonant in the onset of a

---

7. For additional evidence motivating the distinction between two types of long vowels in Turkish, see Kornfilt (1982).
8. The partitive forms in (16) exhibit their t-less allomorph. The full partitive ending ta appears in (17) below as well as in such forms as lohta 'salmon' and maata 'land'. The alternation between ta and a is due to a rule which deletes an intervocalic t following a stressless vowel preceded by a C.

closed syllable.   The following forms,   however, represent a class of apparent counterexamples to this generalization:

Figure 17

	nom.	gen.	part.	iness.	adess.
'grip'	ote	otteen	otetta	otteessa	otteella

As can be seen from the genitive, inessive and adessive forms, the stem must be considered as having a geminate t̠.   There are, however, three anomalies to be seen.   First, the nominative form contains a single t̠, even though the syllable of which it is the onset is an open one.   Second, a long vowel represented here by the double vowel sequence e̠e̠ is seen in the genitive, inessive and adessive forms of (17) but not in the corresponding forms of (16).   Thirdly, the partitive suffix shows an unexpected geminate t̠.

Keyser and Kiparsky (1982) argue that all stems in Finnish are V-final. They further represent stems of the type under consideration here as ending in a CV sequence in which the C is "empty".   Hence, the underlying form of the nominative ote̠ appears as:

Figure 18

The final V-element (and its attendant association line) is deleted by a cyclic rule of e-Deletion which, following Keyser and Kiparsky, operates to delete a syllable final /e/ and the V dominating it.[9] As a result of this rule, a stem final C is produced and, as a result of resyllabification, the final syllable is closed, thereby causing the preceding geminate t̲t̲ to degeminate. The final C, being "empty", will simply not appear on the surface.[10]

This does not mean that this C never surfaces. In fact there is strong evidence which suggests that just this happens when the stem final C is followed by the partitive ending. To see this consider the following representation:

Figure 19

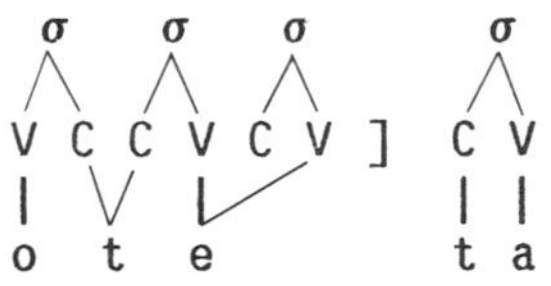

Given this representation, two things will happen. On the first cycle, indicated by the right bracket on the CV-tier, e-Deletion operates to delete the stem final V. Resyllabification then closes the penultimate syllable and the geminate consonant degeminates. On the second cycle the stem final C associates with the initial t̲ of the partitive ending by the conventions of association (5), as indicated in the following figure:

---

9. This rule deletes only the V-element in the case of multiattached vowels such as that of (18). It operates, not only in the nominative case, but elsewhere as well. In what follows we shall be particularly interested in its operation in the partitive case.
10. Finnish, therefore, differs from Turkish in not having a rule associating the final stem vowel with the empty C position.

Figure 20

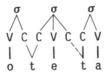

Thus, the stem final C accounts not only for the degemination observed in the nominative and in the partitive but also for the otherwise inexplicable appearance of the partitive ending as -tta.

The stem final C accounts for yet another aspect of these forms. Thus far nothing has been said about the ending in the genitive form otteen. In keeping with the discussion above we suppose an underlying representation as follows:

Figure 21

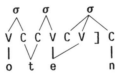

Here e-Deletion fails to apply since the stem final V is not in syllable final position. Moreover, because the syllable following the geminate /t/ is an open syllable, degemination cannot apply. On the second cycle nothing happens to change these configurations and the genitive form surfaces normally, as in:

Figure 22

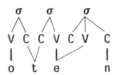

Here, as in the earlier example of the nominative ote, as well as in the Turkish example daa, we see that a C element associated with no segmental material has no surface manifestation. Similar accounts may be given of the inessive and adessive forms.

We see, then, that Finnish provides strong support not only for unassociated elements on the CV tier but for CV representation in general, since it is difficult to see how these various forms of ote could otherwise be accounted for in a phonologically principled way.

3.5 Compensatory Lengthening

The phenomenon of compensatory lengthening is a consequence of spreading as we have characterized it in the previous section. What is distinctive about compensatory lengthening is that it involves spreading to an unoccupied position in the CV-tier that had earlier been occupied by a consonant or vowel. Compensatory lengthening may thus be viewed as involving a "re-timing" of relations within the syllable, word, or (in some cases) phrase, according to which some segments spread to positions left available by other segments.

Preaspiration in Icelandic has been described as a type of compensatory lengthening by Thráinsson (1978). As his findings are highly relevant to the present discussion, we shall summarize them here. In Icelandic, the past tense is formed by means of the suffix t, as shown by the following forms:

Figure 23

	infinitive	past
'untie'	leys-a	leys-t-i
'stare'	glap-a	glap-t-i
'wake'	vak-a	vak-t-i

The first member of a pair of identical voiceless aspirated stops (represented by p̲ t̲ and k̲ in the orthography) is replaced by h̲ as a result of a highly productive rule of the phonology. Thus, for example, the past tense suffix t̲ causes a stem final t̲ to be replaced by h̲:

Figure 24

	infinitive	past	
'meet'	mæt-a	mæt-t-i	[maihtɪ]
'grant'	veit-a	veit-t-i	[veihtɪ]
'utilize'	nyt-a	nyt-t-i	[nihtɪ]

In order to account for these facts, Thráinsson proposes to recognize three separate tiers in Icelandic: one allotted to laryngeal features such as [+ spread glottis] and [-spread glottis], one allotted to supralaryngeal features, and one allotted to the elements C and V. Thráinsson argues that preaspiration is to be regarded as a process deleting the set of supralaryngeal features characterizing the first of two identical voiceless aspirated stops, accompanied by a spreading of the preceding vowel onto the C-element left vacant. This can be schematized as follows, where h̲ represents the feature [+ spread glottis]:

Figure 25

```
        h   h                 h   h                 h   h
        |   |                 |   |                 |   |
    V   C   C  --->   V   C   C  --->   V   C   C
    |   |   |                 |   |                 |  /        |
    a   t   t                 a       t                 a           t
```

Upon deletion of the t̲, the a̲ spreads to the C-element left unoccupied. The result is a long vowel, the second component of which is aspirated. This, of course, is precisely the articulatory description of the phonetic sequence [ah].

As this example shows, the argument for the CV-tier from compensatory lengthening is analogous to the argument for the autosegmental representation of tone from the "stability" of the tonal tier. The phonological reality of the CV-tier is demonstrated by the fact that it retains its identity in spite of processes which delete elements of the segmental tier (or the supralaryngeal tier, as in Thráinsson's example).[11]

3.6 The Mora

Our fourth argument for the CV-tier is based upon the linguistic category "mora". We understand the mora as a unit involved in the determination of syllable weight, such that light syllables count as one mora and heavy syllables count as two. As remarked earlier in Chapter 1, the distinction between light and heavy syllables plays an important role in many languages. For example, in English this distinction is crucial in predicting the placement of stress within a word.

---

11. For extensive discussion of compensatory lengthening in Ancient Greek dialects within a framework related to ours, see Steriade (1982).

Recall that in Chapter 1, we defined heavy and light syllables in terms of units of the CV-tier.   A heavy syllable is one containing a complex (branching) nucleus; and a light syllable is one containing a simple (non-branching) nucleus.   The concept "mora" may be characterized in terms of this distinction as follows:[12]

Figure 26

A mora is any element of the CV-tier dominated by the
node "Nucleus" in the Nucleus display.

We now examine Danish, a language in which the mora plays a particularly significant role. Let us first consider a set of facts suggesting that the syllable functions as a phonological unit in Danish.   As has frequently been observed (see e.g. Stemann 1965, Basbøll 1974), the consonants /p t k d g r/ have the regular variants [b d g ð γ ɹ] in syllable-final position.[13] For example:[14]

Figure 27

a. syllable-initial

/p/	pi:ʔl	<u>pil</u>	'arrow'
/t/	ti:mə	<u>time</u>	'hour'
/k/	kasə	<u>kasse</u>	'box'
/d/	a:dam	<u>Adam</u>	'Adam'
/g/	hugo	<u>Hugo</u>	'Hugo'
/r/	re:ʔn	<u>ren</u>	'clean'

12. In some usages, the term "mora" is confined to languages in which the mora bears tone or pitch accent. We may restrict our definition to reflect this usage by adding the qualification "...that functions as a tone bearing unit" to the definition in (26). The broader definition of the term "mora" as characterized in (26) will be assumed in the present discussion.

13. [γ] is optionally realized as [i], [u], or ∅ by younger speakers and is elided after nasals; [ð] may be elided after sonorants (cf. Basbøll 1974).

14. The ? represents the stød; see discussion below.

b. syllable-final

/p/	ɔbmon?drə	opmuntre	'to cheer up'
/t/	nadsdøgə	natstykke	'night-piece'
/k/	fagtom	faktum	'fact'
/d/	maδ	mad	'food'
/g/	dɔγ	dog	'still'
/r/	smœ̈ʝ	smør	'butter'

The syllable-final variants also occur immediately before unstressed reduced vowels:[15]

Figure 28

/p/	kɔbəʝ	kopper	'smallpox'
/t/	pe:?dəʝ	Peter	'Peter'
/k/	hø:?gəʝ	høker	'grocer'
/d/	re:δə	rede	'nest'
/g/	ba:γə	bage	'bake'

As is already implicit in the characterization given in (27), the allophony of /p t k d g r/ is determined by the position of the consonant within the syllable. In particular, in syllable-final position, a voiceless stop voices, a voiced stop spirantizes and /r/ becomes a glide [ʝ]. As we observe in (28), the same set of variations occurs before unstressed, reduced vowels. These facts can be accounted for naturally if we make the assumption that consonants are ambisyllabic in this environment.[16] We may state the rule of ambisyllabification as follows:

---

15. Reduced vowels are deleted after sonorants. Hence there are no examples of /r/ comparable to the other forms in (28).
16. Such an analysis was earlier suggested by Martinet (1937).

Figure 29- Danish Ambisyllabification

Given this rule, all of the facts discussed above can be subsumed under a single generalization.

Let us turn now to a consideration of the accentual feature known as the stød. The stød is a laryngeal gesture involving a momentary and usually partial constriction of the glottis during the production of a voiced continuant (vowel or consonant).[17] This feature occurs at most once per syllable and its position is determined by the structure of the syllable. If the syllable contains a long vowel, the stød is manifested on the second mora of the vowel; for example, [hu:?s] 'house'. If it contains a short vowel immediately followed by a sonorant or [ð], then the stød is realized on the consonant; for example, [dan?sk] 'Danish'. Finally, if a syllable which might otherwise be expected to have a stød ends in a short vowel plus an obstruent other than [ð], then the stød has no phonetic realization, except in certain Western varieties of standard Danish where a characteristic intonation pattern normally associated with the stød appears. The stød is phonemic in Danish, as is evidenced by such minimal pairs as the following:

Figure 30

a.	man?	mand	'man'
	man	man	'you' (impersonal)
b.	væl?	væld	'spring'

---

17. Our description is based primarily upon the phonetic studies of Lauritsen (1968) and Petersen (1973). Lauritsen has incorrectly transcribed her spectrograms in some cases.

	væl	<u>vel</u>	'well'
c.	klæ:?ɹ	<u>klæder</u>	'becomes, suits'
	klæ:ɹ	<u>klæder</u>	'clothes'

A long vowel in a stød-bearing syllable may be shortened if it is followed in syllable-final position by one of the voiced continuants [δ w ɹ γ] manifesting /d v r g/, respectively. In this case the stød may be moved to the sonorant or [δ]. We thus find variants such as the following:

Figure 31

a.	fo:?δ ~ foδ?	<u>fod</u>	'foot'
b.	dæ:?γ ~ dæγ?	<u>dag</u>	'day'
c.	sbi:?ɹ ~ sbiɹ?	<u>spir</u>	'spire'
d.	sgæ:?w ~ sgæw?	<u>skæv</u>	'slanted'

We have written the stød immediately following the segment with which it coincides phonetically. In each case, therefore, it coincides either with the second half of the long vowel or with the sonorant immediately following the short vowel. A provisional account of the distribution of stød might take the following form: the stød coincides with the second mora of a heavy syllable, where that mora is occupied by a sonorant or [δ].

Now let us consider the occurrence of stød in VCV sequences where the second V is a reduced vowel. On the basis of our previous claim that the first C in such sequences is ambisyllabic, we might expect that a stød will be realized on that consonant under otherwise appropriate circumstances and, in fact, this is the case:

Figure 32

a.	æδ?əɹ	<u>edder</u>	'venom'
b.	man?ən	<u>manden</u>	'the man'
c.	møl?əɹ	<u>møller</u>	'Møller' (proper name)

d.	søm?əð	<u>sømmet</u>	'the nail'
e.	tøm?əɹ	<u>tømmer</u>	'timber'
f.	ven?əɹ	<u>vinder</u>	'wins'

If the second vowel of a VCV sequence is a <u>full</u> vowel, on the other hand, stød never occurs.

The stød assignment rule can now be stated in a simple fashion. Let us assume that in Danish, as in Icelandic, glottal features are arrayed on an independent tier of representation. Symbolizing the features characterizing the stød as ?, we may propose the following, where the dashed line indicates the entry of an association line and the * indicates an accented syllable:

Figure 33 - Stød Association

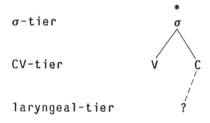

σ-tier

CV-tier

laryngeal-tier

This rule associates the stød ? with the second mora of an accented syllable.[18]

---

18. We assume that a stød associated with an obstruent other than [ð] is deleted by a later rule. Any stød which cannot be associated by (33) is left "floating", and remains unpronounced. The full statement of the alternations between stød and Ø are extremely complex, governed in part by morphological factors. Here we have attempted only to define the phonological contexts in which lexically and grammatically conditioned støds may be phonetically realized.

3.7 Branching Segments

In the earlier literature (see, for example, Hoard 1967, Campbell 1974 among others) a category of <u>complex segments</u> was proposed. This term refers to units (both consonants and vowels) which count phonologically as single segments but which have internal structure comparable to that of sequences of segments. For example, affricates, pre-nasalized stops and diphthongs have been viewed in these terms. As we have seen (Chapter 2), the present approach to syllable structure enables us to characterize such segments in terms of one-many associations between a single element of the CV-tier and a sequence of elements on the segmental tier.

As an illustration of the treatment of complex segments within the present framework, we turn to an example from Spanish.[19] In this language a wide variety of diphthongs arises as a result of sequences of identical vowels occurring both within and across word boundaries. These diphthongs constitute single metrical units, as evidenced by the manner in which they are scanned in Spanish verse (see, for example, Navarro Tomás 1972) The following figure represents the results of these diphthongization processes in two varieties of Spanish. The data from standard Mexican Spanish are taken from Harris (1970) and those from Chicano Spanish from Hutchinson (1974) and Reyes (1976).

---

19. See Keyser and Kiparsky (1982) for further evidence for branching segments in Finnish.

Figure 34

UR	Standard Spanish (fairly rapid speech)	Chicano Spanish (allegretto)
i + i	?	i
i + u	iu̯	iu̯
i + e	ie̯	ie̯
i + o	io̯	io̯
i + a	ia̯	ia̯
u + i	u̯i	u̯i
u + u	?	u
u + e	u̯e	u̯e
u + o	u̯o	u̯o
u + a	u̯a	u̯a
e + i	ei̯	i
e + u	eu̯	iu̯
e + e	?	e
e + o	eo̯	io̯
e + a	ea̯	ia̯
o + i	oi̯	u̯i
o + u	ou̯	u
o + e	oe̯	u̯e
o + o	?	o
o + a	oa̯	u̯a
a + i	ai̯	i
a + u	au̯	u
a + e	ae̯	e
a + o	ao̯	o
a + a	?	a

We have used subscripted arcs to designate vowels which are described as "short". The ? entries indicate gaps in the available information. We have been unable to determine whether like vowel sequences retain some degree of length or reduce to single short vowels in the variety of Spanish described in the first column, but shall assume for the purposes of the following discussion that the first alternative is correct. If the second alternative proves to be correct, however, our description can be modified by the addition of a vowel shortening rule which will have no other consequences for our analysis.

A preliminary analysis of the data in (34) above might lead one to suppose that the following phonological processes are involved: (1) a vowel is shortened before another vowel, (2) a shortened, non-low vowel is raised, (3) a shortened, low vowel is deleted, and (4) a sequence of two identical vowels is simplified to a single vowel. The first of these processes would be common to both varieties of Spanish, while the remaining processes would be characteristic of Chicano allegretto speech alone. For purposes of the discussion we formalize this preliminary hypothesis as follows:

Figure 35

a.   V ---> [+ short] / ___ V

b. $\begin{bmatrix} +short \\ -low \end{bmatrix}$ ---> [+high]

c. $\begin{bmatrix} +short \\ +low \end{bmatrix}$ ---> ∅

d.   [+syl] [+syl] ---> ∅,2   (where 1=2)
        1   2

Upon closer examination, however, we can find a number of problems with this account. First of all, spectrographic evidence reported by Hutchinson (1974) shows that the non-identical vowel sequences of Chicano allegretto style have the duration of single, stressed vowel nuclei, no matter where the stress falls in the input sequence.[20] The shortening rule given as (35a) cannot yield this result since its output will be a shortened vowel followed by a normal vowel, a sequence whose duration will necessarily exceed that of a normal vowel. In order to produce the correct output, it would be necessary to modify (35a) so that both vowels are shortened to the duration of a single vowel.

Secondly, this analysis does not account for the observation that if either input vowel is stressed, the resulting vowel or vowel sequence is stressed. Consider the following examples (orthographic forms are given to the left of the arrow with stresses marked; note that orthographic h is "silent" in Spanish):

.

---

20. Hutchinson (1974, 187) qualifies this statement as follows: "ei and ou sequences act differently. The spectrograms show that if the initial stress configuration consists of two unstressed vowels (VV), the duration of the new syllabic nucleus will be that of a single unstressed vowel." It is worth pointing out, however, that Hutchinson's sampling consists of 52 utterances containing samples of all vowel combinations. Since there are 25 different VV sequences, this sampling (averaging roughly two tokens per sequence) would be too small to provide statistically significant support for this claim.

Figure 36

a. téngo hípo --->   tèŋguípo   'I have the hiccups.'

b. cómo Éva   --->   kòmuéβa   'like Eva'

c. ésta híja   --->   èstíxa   'this daughter'

d. comí uvítas --->   komiùβitas   'I ate grapes.'

e. cortó uvítas--->   kortùβítas   'he cut grapes.'

f. vendrá Inéz --->   bendrinés   'Inez will come.'

In the first set of examples, (36a-c), the initial vowel of the VV sequence is stressless and the second vowel is stressed. In the second set of examples, (36d-f), the initial vowel is stressed and the second vowel is stressless. In both cases the shortening or deletion of the initial vowel results in a sequence in which the second vowel is perceived as the bearer of stress. These facts are not accommodated under the analysis given above.[21]

Thirdly, the rules given in (35) involve an ordering paradox which strongly argues against this analysis. To see this consider sequences of the form /oo/ and /ou/. We must assume that rule (35d) applies before rule (35b) in the case of /oo/ in order to arrive at the correct surface output [o]. However, in the case of /ou/ we must suppose the reverse order to derive the desired [u]. This is illustrated below:

---

21. Hutchinson is aware of this problem and deals with it by the addition of a separate rule to shift accent onto the second vowel of a VV sequence in allegretto speech. There is, however, a generalization which Hutchinson's account misses. Notice that the set of strings affected by the accent shift rule is co-extensive with the set of strings affected by the vowel sandhi rules postulated for vowel sandhi in allegretto style. These rules all have the property that the initial vowel of a two vowel sequence is either deleted or otherwise altered so that it is no longer capable of bearing stress. The fact that stress surfaces on the following vowel should, if possible, follow automatically from the changes that occur in the initial vowel. In the account given in Hutchinson it is merely accidental that the accent shift rule moves the stress to the vowel that "survives" the reduction rules.

Figure 37

a.   /oo/   b.   /ou/
      Ø   by (35d)   u   by (35b)
      -       by (35b)   Ø   by (35d)
     _____   _____
      [o]   output   [u]   output

Apparently, (35d) applies wherever it can in a derivation. This behavior cannot be explained under generally accepted principles of rule interaction.

Clearly, one or another (or all) of these deficiencies could be dealt with by the addition of further rules or ad hoc principles of rule application and the like. However, the fact that we have to have recourse to such alternatives is in itself prima facie evidence that the linear approach fails to characterize these processes correctly. We turn now to a solution to these problems, elaborating on certain ideas suggested by Reyes (1976).

To begin with, let us recall the observation, made earlier, that vowel sequences across word boundaries normally constitute single rhythmic units in all varieties of Spanish. We postulate that this rhythmic unit is the foot, a category of metrical analysis which is hierarchically superordinate to the elements of the syllable tier. Feet are formed according to the following principles, which hold for all varieties of Spanish:[22]

Figure 38 - Foot Construction

a. A C-initial syllable constitutes the left branch of a foot.

b. A V-initial syllable constitutes the left branch of a

---

22. We have stated (38a-c) as language specific principles. However, it seems likely that (38c), unlike the others, is a universal principle which does not need to be stated as part of Spanish phonology. The unit "foot" under consideration here should not be identified with the foot discussed in Harris (1983), which is a higher ranking prosodic unit than the unit under discussion here.

of the same foot as the preceding syllable.

c. A foot is stressed iff it dominates a syllable which is stressed.

In terms of these principles (36d) will have the following foot structure prior to the sandhi processes applying in Chicano speech:

Figure 39

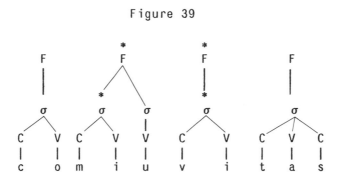

In addition to these pan-hispanic principles of foot construction, Chicano allegretto style is characterized by three additional rules. The first of these simplifies any sequence of two consecutive V-elements by deleting the second and reassociating the remaining vowel to the first:

Figure 40 - V Degemination (Chicano allegretto)

(The symbols x and y are to be understood as variables ranging over single segments of the segmental tier.) (40) creates a diphthong which, by virtue of being dominated by a single V, constitutes a single timing unit.[23] It is this rule that accounts for the observation by Hutchinson cited earlier, according to which vowel sequences in Chicano allegretto style have the same duration as single vowels.

To complete our description of Chicano allegretto style, we need two additional rules, one that accounts for the raising of mid vowels to high vowels, and another that accounts for the deletion of low vowels. These rules may be defined upon the diphthongal configurations created by rule (40), as follows:

Figure 41 - Mid Vowel Raising (Chicano allegretto)

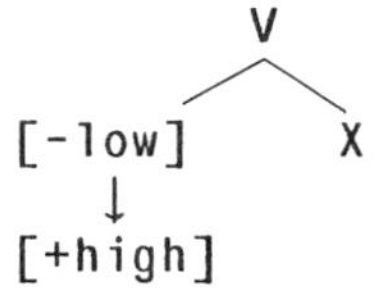

```
            V
           / \
   [-low]     X
     ↓
   [+high]
```

Figure 42 - Low Vowel Deletion (Chicano allegretto)

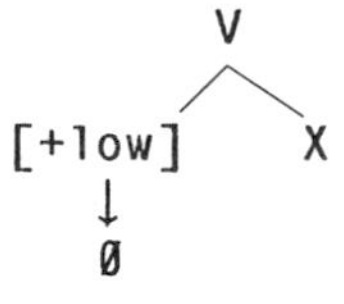

```
            V
           / \
   [+low]     X
     ↓
     Ø
```

We illustrate these rules with the following derivation of the consecutive vowel sequence of example (36a):

---

23. (40) is formulated in a maximally simple fashion, deleting the second of two V-elements occurring anywhere in a phonological representation. It may be, however, that this rule will need to be modified in an appropriate way to prevent its application to heterosyllabic, word-internal sequences such as those of bahía 'bay' or aún 'yet'. Since it is unclear at this point exactly what modification will be involved, we provisionally leave (40) as it stands.

Figure 43

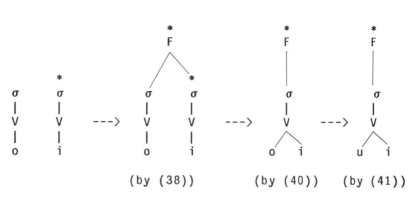

(by (38))   (by (40))   (by (41))

(We assume that σ-nodes which do not dominate other elements are deleted by convention. This accounts for the loss of the second σ-node in the third stage of the derivation in (43).)

Returning to the set of problems noted earlier, we have already seen that under the present account, the problem of duration inherent in the linear account no longer exists. This is because the application of (40) turns a sequence of segments associated with two separate timing units into a sequence of segments associated with a single timing unit, thereby accounting for the durational relationships noted by Hutchinson.[24]

The second problem raised by the linear account concerns the shifting of stress onto the vowel which survives the processes of vowel reduction. Recall that this shift should follow automatically as a consequence of the vowel sandhi rules, but cannot in a linear account. In terms of the hierarchical framework given above, however, stress shift follows automatically. We assume that stress (indicated by *) is a property of the

---

24. It should be noted that this analysis says nothing about the shortening process reported for standard Spanish whereby the first member of a two-vowel sequence is said to be shortened with respect to the second. Assuming that these facts can be confirmed by instrumental investigation, they are in all probability best treated in terms of the phonetic component, which specifies phonetic vowel duration as a function of vowel height, contextual features and the like. It seems reasonable to think such specifications do not interact with phonological processes of the type described above.

syllable tier in Spanish and is assigned by an independent set of rules. Once stress is assigned, it percolates upwards to the F node in accordance with (38c). At this level, stress will be preserved no matter what processes may operate to delete elements on the syllable tier.

We turn now to the third problem, involving the apparent ordering paradox illustrated in (37). After Foot Construction (38) applies, the underlying sequences /oo/ and /ou/ have the following shapes:

Figure 44

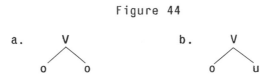

These configurations, as we have seen, describe vowel sequences which constitute single timing units. From this point of view the first configuration (44a) presents a representation which is phonetically indistinguishable from the following:

Figure 45

The question which is of interest here is whether there is a phonological difference between (44a) and (45) or whether they are, in fact, simply notational variants of one another. Our first observation is that both of these representations can have only one phonetic interpretation: that of a phonological unit having the quality of the vowel /o/ and occupying a single unit of timing. Our second observation is that representations like (44a) and (45) never appear to be differentiated by phonological rules: phonological rules always act as if the simpler of the two representations, that is, (45), were present. On the basis of these observations we propose the following universal convention on phonological representations:

Figure 46 - Twin Sister Convention

Twin sisters degeminate.

This convention, which is defined on melody units (autosegments) only, applies whenever the relevant configuration arises.[25]

This convention provides the solution to the ordering paradox discussed earlier. The Twin Sister Convention (46) applies automatically to the output of V Degemination to convert representation (44a) into (45), thereby bleeding the operation of Mid Vowel Raising (41). This rule, however, can still apply to (44b), converting this representation into the following:

Figure 47

To this representation the Twin Sister Convention applies, simplifying the like vowel sequence to the single vowel [u]. We are thus able to account for the facts of Spanish vowel degemination solely in terms of principles that are independently motivated in phonological theory.

---

25. This convention is widely assumed in autosegmental studies of tone: see, for example, Elimelech (1978). A similar convention is invoked by Harris in his recent study of Spanish plural formation (Harris 1980). For evidence that the Twin Sister Convention does not apply when one of the two identical autosegments is associated with a second element on the related tier, see Kisseberth (1901).

3.8 French Liaison and the Feature [+syllabic]

In this section we turn to a consideration of French liaison from the point of view of the three-tiered model of the syllable developed up to this point. We attempt to show that within this framework there is a natural account of French liaison which is not available in linear terms. We also show that the facts which led Chomsky and Halle (1968) to postulate a feature [+syllabic] receive a simple reinterpretation within this framework.

Consider the following examples of French liaison drawn from Chomsky and Halle (1968, 353ff):

Figure 48

Consonants	Liquids	Vowels	Glides
petiʎ garçon	petiʎ livre	petit enfant	petit oiseau
cher garcon	cher livre	cher enfant	cher oiseau
le garçon	le livre	leʎ enfant	leʎ oiseau
pareil gâchis	pareil livre	vieil ami	vieil oiseau

These forms illustrate the well-known linking phenomena in French whereby a word-final consonant deletes preceding a word which begins with an obstruent or a liquid, and a word-final vowel deletes preceding a word which begins with a vowel or a glide. In order to capture this phenomenon Schane (1968) proposed the following relatively straightforward rule:

Figure 49 - Liaison (Schane)

$$\begin{bmatrix} -\alpha voc \\ \alpha cons \end{bmatrix} \quad \text{---}> \quad \emptyset \; / \; \underline{\hspace{1.5em}} \; \# \; [\alpha con]$$

This rule was based on the assumption that <u>consonantal</u> and <u>vocalic</u> were distinctive feature categories that specified the classes of consonants, vowels, liquids and glides as follows:

Figure 50

	Consonants	Liquids	Vowels	Glides
cons	+	+	-	-
voc	-	+	+	-

However, as Milner (1967) showed, Schane's solution runs into difficulties when one considers the behavior of glide-initial loanwords in French. Thus, yogi and whisky trigger deletion of a preceding consonant in les̸ yogis or peti̸ whisky while they fail to trigger elision of a preceding vowel in le yogi and le whisky. If Schane's rule is to be maintained, these forms would require an additional rule of liaison restricted just to foreign words:

Figure 51 - Liaison (Foreign Words)

1. $\begin{bmatrix} +voc \\ -cons \end{bmatrix}$ ---> $\emptyset$ / ___ # $\begin{bmatrix} +voc \\ -cons \end{bmatrix}$

2. $\begin{bmatrix} -voc \\ +cons \end{bmatrix}$ ---> $\emptyset$ / ___ # $\begin{Bmatrix} [-voc] \\ [+cons] \end{Bmatrix}$

These two rules are clearly undesirable because they cannot be collapsed. To overcome this difficulty Milner and C.J. Bailey suggested that the distinctive feature category syllabic be substituted for the category vocalic. This suggestion gives rise to the following characterization of the major classes of speech sounds:

Figure 52

	sonorant	syllabic	consonantal
vowels	+	+	−
liquids	+	−	+
nasals	+	−	+
glides	+	−	−
obstruents	−	−	+

In terms of this division of features it is possible to replace (51) with a rule sensitive to the feature category <u>syllabic</u> as follows (Chomsky and Halle 1968, 355):[26]

Figure 53 - Liaison (Chomsky and Halle 1968)

$$\begin{bmatrix} -\alpha syl \\ \alpha cons \end{bmatrix} \text{---> } \emptyset \text{ / \_\_\_\_ \# } \begin{bmatrix} -\alpha syl \\ +foreign \end{bmatrix}$$

This rule enables glides to be classed with liquids and consonants and allows all three to be opposed to vowels. This is precisely the division required to deal with loanwords in French. Moreover, it allows an additional simplification. If one supposes (as suggested by Milner 1973) that there are no underlying word-initial glides in native French words, then one can eliminate the diacritic feature [+foreign] from (53) altogether and assume that the rule applies before a subsequent rule which forms glides out of initial vowels in prevocalic position. Thus, the underlying forms of <u>yogi</u> and

---

26. This rule, as it stands, will delete liquids, nasals, and obstruents before vowels and glides. It therefore differs from (51) which did not apply to liquids. In fact, as we shall see in the following discussion, the truncation rule should apply only to obstruents and some instances of /r/.

whisky will contain initial glides, while native words like oiseau and yeux will be underlyingly vowel-initial. Consequently, rule (53) will treat the latter two words as if they were vowel-initial, blocking consonant deletion and triggering vowel elision. On the other hand, the rule will treat the former two words as containing initial glides, triggering consonant deletion and blocking vowel elision. Most importantly, Rule (49) can now be eliminated from the grammar as its function is entirely subsumed by (53) as revised.

Despite the evident simplicity of this solution, there are certain problems which suggest that it is not correct. To begin with, the truncation rule, as mentioned in footnote 26, should not apply to laterals or to nasals. This latter point requires some discussion, due to the apparent fact that nasals show the same pattern of truncation as obstruents:

Figure 54

Consonants	Liquids	Vowels	Glides
boɴ garçon	boɴ livre	bon ami	bon oiseau

(where a vowel is nasalized before a truncated consonant)

As suggested by the distribution in (54), nasal truncation operates in exactly the same set of environments as liaison (cf. (48) above). Moreover, nasal truncation has the same pattern of behavior with respect to glide-initial loanwords. The following are illustrative:

Figure 55

foreign   native

<u>bon yougoslave</u> [bɔ̃jugɔslav]   <u>bon hiatus</u> [bɔnjatys]

<u>petit yougoslave</u> [pətijugɔslav]   <u>petit hiatus</u> [pətitjatys]

<u>bon whisky</u> [bɔ̃wiski]   <u>bon oiseau</u> [bɔnwazo]

<u>petit whisky</u> [pətiwiski]   <u>petit oiseau</u> [pətitwazo]

Notice also that nasals, like obstruents (see below), are truncated in absolute final position; for example, <u>c'est un bon</u> [bɔ̃]. It would be tempting to regard nasal truncation as the same phenomenon as obstruent truncation. However, nasal truncation is a more general rule than obstruent truncation, applying not only word finally but also word internally, as in <u>bon</u> [bɔ̃], <u>bonté</u> [bɔ̃te] (compare <u>saint</u> [sɛ̃], <u>sainteté</u> [sɛ̃tte]). Moreover, word final nasal truncation is almost entirely restricted to /n/; final /m/ is truncated only in the case of <u>nom</u> [nɔ̃] (cf. <u>nommer</u>), <u>parfum</u> [parfɛ̃] (cf. <u>parfumer</u>). We therefore conclude that nasal truncation should not be collapsed with obstruent truncation, in spite of the similarity of their conditioning.

More importantly, French also contains a rule which deletes consonants in absolute final position. In the phrase <u>c'est un petit</u>, for example, the phrase-final t deletes. The fact that French contains two rules of consonant deletion, one which deletes a consonant before another consonant and another which deletes a consonant in absolute final position, suggests that we are dealing with a syllable-conditioned rule. Notice that while these truncation rules hold for a large portion of the French lexicon, there is an important set of words which never undergoes them. This set of words includes nouns, adjectives and numerals; for example, among the nouns are <u>bec</u>, <u>flic</u>, <u>club</u>, <u>type</u>, <u>échec</u> and <u>chef</u>; among the adjectives are <u>chic</u>, <u>brave</u>, <u>sec</u>, <u>juste</u>, <u>timide</u>, and <u>sage</u>; and among the numerals are <u>sept</u>, neuf and onze.[27] What is significant about these words for our present discussion is that they are exceptions to <u>both</u> truncation rules. Thus, an analysis treating phrase-final truncation as distinct from phrase-internal truncation is unable to account for the fact that any word that is an exception to one is an exception to the other.

Thus, we are faced with the following dilemma. If we take the consonant-final shapes of the truncating words as their underlying representation, the truncation rule will have a large number of exceptions in the native vocabulary of the language. If, on the other hand, we take the vowel-final shapes as underlying and insert the appropriate consonants by an epenthesis rule, then we will be unable to predict which consonant will be inserted on phonological grounds. Moreover, we will be faced with a small number of exceptions consisting of vowel final words to which epenthesis never applies (<u>joli</u>, <u>fichu</u>, <u>vrai</u>, <u>demi</u>, <u>sacré</u>).

The germ of a solution to this problem is contained in the following comment by Malmberg (1972, 140):

> Au point de vue fonctionnel, on peut regarder les
> consonnes de liaison comme des phonèmes latents
> qui demandent certaines conditions pour se réaliser.

How, exactly, might we characterize the notion "latent phoneme"? Intuitively we are dealing with an element of the underlying representation of a word which may be "phonetically realized" only if it can be assigned to a syllable, failing which it simply does not appear. Readers familiar with the literature on stress systems will recognize a similarity between this notion and that of "extrametrical elements" - elements which, while belonging to underlying representations, are idiosyncratically marked with a feature which excludes them from the domain within which prosodic rules, such as rules of stress assignment, apply (cf. Hayes 1981). In metrical

---

27. The fact that some of these items end in orthographic e does not reflect any systematic difference in their phonological behavior.

representations, for example, such elements are unassociated with higher level tree structure.

We propose to treat the truncating obstruents (as well as the truncating /r/) in a similar manner. These consonants will be present in the underlying representation of a word, but, unlike other segments, they will be marked by a feature which excludes them from the domain of core syllabification. These segments will become associated with σ nodes by rule in certain contexts. The most general of these contexts is the "liaison" context - roughly, the position before a vowel-initial word belonging to the same syntactic unit (for further discussion, see Selkirk (1974)). We may now distinguish among such minimally distinct forms as <u>don</u> 'gift', <u>don(t)</u> 'of which' and <u>donc</u> 'therefore' as follows:

Figure 56

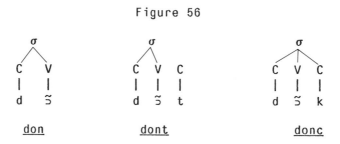

By the rule of Liaison, a consonant is linked to the syllable node dominating an immediately following vowel, providing the appropriate syntactic conditions are satisfied. This rule introduces the association lines accounting for both instances of Liaison in the phrase <u>dont un ami</u> 'whose friend':

Figure 57

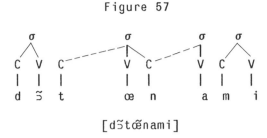

[dɔ̃tæ̃nami]

Note that Liaison affects both extrasyllabic and fully syllabified consonants; we assume that derived ambisyllabic segments, such as the [n] in (57), are subsequently (or perhaps simultaneously) disassociated from the syllable to their left. Finally, "latent" (extrasyllabic) consonants which do not undergo Liaison are deleted by a context-free rule, to be stated below.

We propose the following generalizations about the distribution of extrasyllabic segments in the lexicon:

Figure 58

a. only obstruents and /r/ may be extrasyllabic.

b.   noun and verb stems (roots plus derivational endings) never terminate in extrasyllabic consonants.

c. otherwise, word-final consonants may or may not be extrasyllabic.[28]

(58a) expresses the fact that sonorants other than /r/ never undergo truncation:[29] this follows in our account from the fact that they are always associated with a σ node. (58b) expresses the fact that consonants that are

---

28. The rules determining which word final consonants are extrasyllabic are subtle and complex, varying with speaker and with speech style. For one (largely prescriptive) account see Fouché (1959), whom we follow below.

29. Nasals, as mentioned above, are truncated syllable finally by an independent rule.

members of noun and verb stems never undergo truncation.[30] Finally, (58c) reflects the fact that in all cases except those enumerated in (58a-b), word-final consonants may or may not undergo truncation depending upon the lexical item in question (compare <u>dont</u> and <u>donc</u>).

The following examples, drawn from <u>style soutenu</u>, illustrate (58b,c) above:

Figure 59

a. il prend un train.   'he takes a train.'

b. il prenait un train.   'he took a train.'

Figure 60

a. un marchand italien   'an Italian tradesman'

b. des marchands italiens   'Italian tradesmen'

In such examples, we see that stem final consonants regularly truncate, while inflectional endings may undergo liaison.

The rules accounting for Liaison and Truncation can be formulated as follows:

Figure 61 - Liaison

(under appropriate syntactic conditions)

---

30. Exceptions to this generalization consist of a few nouns which occur in common or fixed expressions, such as <u>nuit</u> 'night' occurring in <u>nuit et jour</u> 'night and day', where liaison is possible for some speakers.

Figure 62 - Consonant Truncation

C' ---> Ø

Figure 63 - Vowel Elision

$$\begin{matrix} V \\ | \\ \partial \end{matrix} ~ ---> ~ Ø ~ / ~ \underline{\hspace{2em}} ~ V$$

We formulate Liaison as a rule linking a C-element to the syllable node dominating a following V-element. Consonant Truncation and Vowel Elision are stated as separate rules, the first of which deletes an extrasyllabic consonant (indicated by the prime) context freely and the second of which deletes schwa before a following V-element.[31] We assume, finally, a rule of Glide Formation as mentioned earlier, which is ordered after the rules of Liaison and Truncation and which operates to turn /uazo/ into [wazo] 'bird'.

We now turn to some further consequences of our analysis. We begin by considering some problems noted by Schane (1978) for a syllable-based analysis of French, and show that these problems do not arise within the present framework. Schane considers a formulation of Consonant Truncation according to which a consonant is deleted before a syllable boundary. Such a rule could be formulated as follows:

Figure 64

C ----> Ø / \underline{\hspace{3em}} $

where $ = syllable boundary

---

31. The reader will observe that we have not introduced boundaries such as (#(#)) in the statement of our rules of Liaison and Truncation. It seems likely that the rules we are discussing refer in part to hierarchical aspects of syntactic organization and may involve a category by category listing of contexts. For related discussion involving Italian see Napoli and Nespor (1979).

Schane observes that such a rule would apply incorrectly to delete word-internal consonants in words such as acteur [aktœr]. In the present analysis, however, such a problem does not arise since the rule of Consonant Truncation does not apply to syllable-final consonants, but rather to unassociated C-elements, which are restricted in occurrence to word-final position by the principles of (58). Notice that our analysis has a further advantage over a syllable boundary approach in the treatment of words such as respect [rɛspɛ], aspect [aspɛ], and suspect [syspɛ], which contrast with words such as direct [dirɛkt], correct [kɔrɛkt], and intellect [ɛ̃tɛllɛkt] in that the orthographic sequence ct is not pronounced in the former. That these words have final consonants in their underlying representation, however, is shown by such related words as respecter, aspectuel, and suspecter, in which the orthographic ct is pronounced. Under an analysis incorporating rule (64), all the items in the much larger class of words including direct, correct and intellect must be marked as exceptions. Furthermore, the stems respect, aspect and suspect must also be marked as exceptional just in case an affix follows, in order to account for the phonetic [k] in forms like respecter. In the present analysis, on the other hand, the three items respect, aspect, and suspect are represented with final unassociated consonants. When suffixes are added, these consonants are no longer word-final; hence (by the principles stated earlier) they cannot be extrasyllabic.

A second problem raised by Schane involves the treatment of irregular forms such as the numeral six. The final consonant of this word undergoes truncation in liaison contexts before consonant-initial words, appears as [z] in liaison contexts before vowel-initial words, and appears as [s] in non-liaison contexts:

Figure 65

```
si[∅]    garçons              'six boys'
si[z]    amis                 'six friends'
si[s]    arrivent             'six arrive'
si[s]    (pre-pausally)       'six'
```

The problem here is that while six is an exception to Schane's Consonant Truncation given in (64), it is only partly so, since it undergoes Truncation regularly in liaison environments. There is no principled way of accounting for this partial exceptionality within a framework incorporating (64).

Once again this problem does not arise within the present approach. Assuming that the underlying shape of this word is /sis/, we mark this word as undergoing the following minor rule, ordered after Liaison:[32]

Figure 66

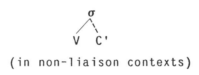

(in non-liaison contexts)

To account for the [z] of si[z] amis, we assume a minor rule of intervocalic voicing which is restricted to the numerals six, dix and, in some styles, neuf.

Thirdly, Schane calls attention to the problem raised by words beginning with h-aspiré. This consists of a class of words which begin with phonetic vowels, but which behave phonologically as if they began with consonants. The following data are illustrative:

---

32. This rule also applies variably as a major rule in liaison contexts, for some speakers, where it takes precedence over (61).

Figure 67

petiƚ	héros	'little hero'
boⁿ	héros	'good hero'
siX	héros	'six heroes'
l[ə]	héros	'the hero'
nouveau	héros	'new hero'
beau	héros	'handsome hero'

The first three forms demonstrate that final consonants (both oral and nasal) truncate before héros. The fourth form demonstrates that ə is not elided before héros. The fifth and sixth forms show that adjectives with suppletive forms assume their pre-consonantal shape before héros. As Schane points out, these forms are problematical for a treatment making use of syllable boundaries since the underlying representation of petit héros is identical, with respect to syllabification, to petit ami. Consequently, words like héros must be marked in some arbitrary way to distinguish them from other vowel-initial words.

In the framework developed here, it is quite natural to suppose that the so-called h-aspiré is represented as a C-element of syllable structure which dominates no consonant on the segmental tier. Thus, héros is, under this assumption, represented as follows:

Figure 68

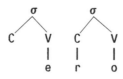

In this way our analysis accounts for the phonological behavior associated with h-aspiré words without requiring the introduction of special rules or diacritic features. Moreover, it does so by making use of a device which has been independently motivated in our earlier discussions of Finnish and Turkish; namely, the use of C-elements which are unassociated with elements on the segmental tier.[33]

Our analysis is similar in certain respects to the "abstract" analysis of h-aspiré words proposed by Selkirk and Vergnaud (1973). In their analysis, the fact that h-aspiré words behave phonologically as if they began with a consonant is explained by attributing an initial /h/ to their underlying representation. This segment is deleted after all other phonological rules have applied. Our approach is similar to theirs in that it treats both h-aspiré words and consonant-initial words as identical in the relevant respect; namely, words of both types begin with C-elements. However, unlike Selkirk and Vergnaud, we are not constrained to assign any specific identity to the initial C-element of h-aspiré words. In this respect our analysis is not abstract at all since we postulate no segment underlyingly which is not also present at the surface.[34]

More recently, however, a number of phonologists have argued that h-aspiré words should not be treated as consonant-initial words at all, but rather as vowel-initial words identical in their underlying representation to other vowel-initial words in French. The idiosyncratic behavior of h-aspiré words is accounted for, under such proprosals, by assigning them a set of diacritic features marking them as exceptions to each of the rules which they fail to undergo.

These approaches are motivated by the justifiable desire to avoid excessive abstractness in underlying representations. However, there are a number of problems with such approaches which we do not believe have been adequately dealt with in the relevant literature. First of all, in order to mark h-aspiré words as exceptions to rules, it is necessary to formulate the

---

33. This analysis of h-aspiré words has been independently suggested by Morris Halle.
34. These arguments generalize, as noted earlier, to the analysis of Finnish and Turkish.

relevant rules in such a way that the words in question satisfy their structural descriptions. Take, for example, the treatment of consonant truncation, which has traditionally been formulated as follows:

Figure 69

$$C \longrightarrow \emptyset \; / \; \rule{1cm}{0.4pt} \; (\#) \quad \left\{ \begin{array}{c} \# \\ C \end{array} \right\}$$

This rule, as we have seen, applies not only before consonant-initial words but before h-aspiré words as well. Thus, it applies, for example, before a word like héros. However, if h-aspiré words are treated underlyingly as vowel-initial, there is no straightforward way to account for this fact by a rule like (69). Partly to solve this problem, Klausenberger (1978) suggests that truncating words like petit be represented as vowel-final underlyingly, and that consonant truncation be reformulated as a rule of consonant insertion, as follows:

Figure 70

$$\emptyset \longrightarrow C \; / \; \rule{1cm}{0.4pt} \; (\#)V$$

Words like héros can now simply be marked as context exceptions to this rule.

There is no way of predicting which consonant is to be inserted in any given case without a further and highly complex elaboration of the rule feature analysis. This is not a "pseudo-problem", as Klausenberger suggests (1978, 28). He states: "It can simply be asserted that whatever means is used to determine the underlying final consonant, in the deletion analysis, may also be employed in deciding which consonant must be inserted." The means used in the deletion analysis to determine the identity of the underlying final consonant in words like _petit_ is simply scansion of the underlying representation. Since the underlying representation does not contain a t̲ in Klausenberger's analysis, inspection of it can reveal nothing. Thus, we are unable to agree that this is a pseudo-problem but rather raise it again, with Schane (1973), as a serious problem for this type of analysis.

A second problem for "concrete" analyses of h-aspiré words, first pointed out by Selkirk and Vergnaud, is the fact that this set of words, while varying in membership from speaker to speaker, behaves consistently like consonant-initial words with respect to all the relevant rules of the phonology. Thus, we do not find in the speech of single speakers examples of h-aspiré words which behave like vowel-initial words with respect to some rules and like consonant-initial words with respect to others. For example, taking the set of forms given in (67) as our basis for comparison, no speaker exhibits sets of forms like the following:

Figure 71

a.　petiƚ　héros
　　l[ə]　héros
　　nouveau héros
b.　si[z]　héros
　　bel　héros
　　bon　héros

This fact follows automatically from any analysis that postulates an underlying initial consonant, whether "abstract" as in the Selkirk and Vergnaud analysis, or non-abstract as in ours. But it does not follow from an analysis that treats h-aspiré words as vowel-initial. By normal processes of historical loss, we should expect some exception features to be eliminated and others retained, creating sets of data such as that given in (71) above.

In the face of this argument, a proponent of the concrete analysis may take one of two positions. The first is to deny that the facts are as stated above, claiming that data sets such as that given in (71) are, in fact, attestable in the speech of single speakers. The second is to acknowledge the correctness of the facts as stated above, and introduce a novel mechanism in support of the analysis. Both positions have, in fact, been taken in the recent literature. Tranel (1981, 299) argues for the former. His evidence consists solely of a discussion of the word hameçon 'hook' as it occurs in the expression mordre à l'hameçon 'nibble at the bait'. According to his source, all speakers use the elided form of the article in the latter expression, but divide as to whether the word hameçon triggers consonant truncation elsewhere. This observation, however, cannot be taken as evidence against our claim that h-aspiré words behave uniformly with respect to all relevant phonological rules. One can cite numerous instances of words which have idiosyncratic pronunciations in certain fixed expressions. For example, many speakers of American English who ordinarily use the article a before h-initial words use the form an before the single lexical item historical, pronouncing the latter without an h initially. Nonetheless, they will pronounce historical with an initial h in all other contexts. It is reasonable to suppose that these speakers delete the initial h just in the sequence an historical. A similar account is sufficient to explain the behavior of hameçon. What would be required to falsify the claim that hameçon behaves consistently for any given speaker with regard to French phonological rules would be to show, for example, that hameçon regularly takes the elided form of the definite article (l'hameçon) but the truncated form of the indefinite article (u(n) hameçon) in all contexts in which these words may occur, in the speech of a single speaker. We know of no facts leading us to suppose that this is the case. We conclude that Tranel's observation provides no evidence in favor of treating h-aspiré words as vowel-initial.

The second approach is taken by Gaatone (1978) and Klausenberger (1978), both of whom agree that the facts are correct as we have characterized them but who attempt to accommodate these facts by introducing a novel theoretical device, which we might term the "umbrella" feature. Such features serve to express the exceptionality of a form not to one but to a set of rules, which need have no formal properties in common, other than, as in the present case, that of applying across word boundaries before vowel initial words. In the case of the analyses proposed by Gaatone and Klausenberger, this feature (which is named [-vowel] by Klausenberger and [-sandhi context] by Gaatone) expresses the exceptionality of h-aspiré words to all rules which otherwise apply in this context. The difficulty with this theoretical move should be obvious: it treats as accidental the fact that the set of rules subsumed under the "umbrella" feature all share a single phonological property, that of mentioning vowels as their righthand context. In sum, an "umbrella" feature does not explain the phenomenon under discussion but merely provides a label for it.[35]

To summarize, in this section we have postulated an analysis of liaison and truncation phenomena which involves the syllabification principles of (58) and the following rules:

---

35. We have not mentioned one respect in which h-aspiré words are often said to differ from consonant-initial words. H-aspiré words, according to this widely cited tradition, preserve immediately preceding ∂s from deletion in circumstances where they would otherwise delete: for example, cette [sɛt∂] hache 'this ax' versus cette [sɛt] tache 'this stain'. Our own investigations have led us to believe that the phonetic facts in question are more complex and variable than traditional descriptions suggest. In the absence of reliable phonetic data, we will not propose an account of this phenomenon here.

Figure 72

Liaison 61
Rule 66
Vowel Elision 63
Consonant Truncation 62

These rules may be ordered as given. We conclude that French does not offer motivation for the feature category <u>syllabic</u>, but does provide strong support for a theory incorporating the syllable framework proposed here.

Chapter 4: Extrasyllabicity and Vowel Epenthesis in Klamath

4.1 Introduction

In the preceding chapters we have developed and motivated a theory of syllable representation which characterizes the syllable as a three-tiered structure having the formal properties of an autosegmental system. We have claimed that the terminal elements of syllable trees are not vowels and consonants themselves, but rather the units of the CV-tier which define positions in syllable structure that particular consonants and vowels may occupy. As we have seen, the independence of the CV-tier and the segmental tier is evidenced by the fact that phonological rules may apply independently to the members of either tier, or may affect the manner in which the elements of these two tiers are associated with each other. Moreover, phonological rules may be sensitive to the difference between otherwise identical syllable trees which differ in the composition of the CV-tier. We take these results as strong evidence in favor of the view we have put forward here.

In this and the next chapter we shall apply this theory to an examination of certain problems in the phonology of Klamath, an American Indian language of Oregon generally classified in the Penutian phylum. Klamath is a language marked by an extraordinary degree of complexity at the level of surface alternations. However, this surface complexity can be shown to derive from the interaction of a fairly small number of phonological rules which operate with great generality throughout the language. Due to the richness of its phonology, this language has been the subject of a number of earlier studies, including those of Kisseberth (1973a,b) and Kean (1973,1974). This earlier work raised a number of problems concerning the nature of rule interaction that, in the opinion of some linguists, remained without a satisfactory solution (White 1973, Thomas 1974, Feinstein and Vago 1981). More recently, it has been suggested that a syllable-based approach of the type developed here might prove successful in dealing with some of these problems (Clements and Keyser 1980, Ter Mors 1981a,b).

As we shall see in what follows, many of the phonological processes of Klamath are optimally stated in terms of syllable structure. In our view, this is not accidental. We have assumed that the syllable structure of a language is characterized in terms of a fairly small number of parameters, as outlined in our earlier chapters. These parameters include the determination of whether a given language is a Type I, II, III or IV language at the level of core syllable representation, whether consonant and vowel clusters are permitted, what the domain of syllabification is, and whether (and where) the Resyllabification Convention is applicable, among others. We further assume that a selection among these parameters can be made in a relatively straightforward manner on the basis of a preliminary analysis of the language data. Thus, for example, extremely simple observations are sufficient to determine whether a given language is a Type I, II, III or IV language, whether consonant clusters are permitted, and so forth. These choices can be integrated in a straightforward way into a theory of "markedness" according to which simpler formal structures represent the less marked choices, to be selected unless there is positive evidence to the contrary.

It is obvious, therefore, that syllable structure provides an organizational principle which permits a significant degree of simplification in the task of the language learner. Syllable structure is a readily discoverable principle of classification which allows the formulation of phonological rules in terms of language-particular classes of sounds such as "syllable-final consonant", "syllabic nucleus", "extrasyllabic sonorant" and the like. Once the principles of syllabic organization have been worked out for a given language, many formally arbitrary rule statements can be replaced by internally-motivated statements involving syllable-based categories such as these. There is, indeed, much reason to suppose that syllable structure is not only a formal category of linguistic organization but also a cognitive reality as well, involved in the storage, accessing, production, and perception of words and phrases, having the effect of coding phoneme sequences into larger units which are themselves the domain of other phonological processes such as those that determine stress and intonation contours. In the case of Klamath, while we know of no direct phonetic documentation of the role of syllable structure in this language, it is not surprising, given these considerations, to find persuasive evidence in favor of the syllable in the phonological rule system itself. It is to this evidence that we now turn.

4.2 Core Syllable Representation

To establish that Klamath is a Type II language, it is sufficient to make the following observations. First, this language has no words which begin with vowels. Second, this language has closed syllables; that is, words ending in consonants or consonant sequences. The single item [gos] 'swan', for example, establishes the second fact. These are, to be sure, surface phenomena which do not necessarily correspond to properties of underlying representation. Nevertheless, it is plausible to suppose that the initial hypotheses of the learner will be constructed on the basis of surface and near-surface forms, to be relinquished only when contradicted by further evidence.

Having established the core syllable typology of Klamath, we must next attempt to determine whether clusters are possible in initial or final position. Our task has been facilitated by the distributional charts showing permissable surface sequences of consonants given in Barker's Klamath Grammar (1964). The following examples illustrate clusters in initial, final and medial position in the word, respectively. First of all, word-initial clusters consist of at most two members in which sonorants and obstruents can occur freely:[1]

Figure 1

a.   obstruent - sonorant

      sla:mitk   'widower'   D,373

      tweqa   'bores through'   D,414

      qnaci:qa   'winks'   D,331

      gmocətk   'old person'   D,145

      dlelGa   'starts'   D,118

b.   obstruent - obstruent

      tqopo: 'thumb'   D,413

      kteWca   'spanks'   D,195

      qpala   'doubles up a fist'   D,324

      tsa:ka   'is light'   D,413

      sdo   'road'   D,358

c.   sonorant - obstruent

      ntopa   'rots'   D,272

      msəs   'prairie dog'   D,243

      ltewa   'eats tules'   D,225

d.   sonorant - sonorant

      mna:ls   'them' (intensive)   D,59

      lwəyqa   'pl. laugh'   D,226

      lmena   'thunders'   D,219

---

1. All examples are taken from Barker's 1963 <u>Klamath Dictionary</u> and his 1964 <u>Klamath Grammar</u>; page references are given to the right of each example. Schwa has two sources in Klamath. First, it is introduced by the rule of Vowel Reduction which we discuss in Chapter 5. Secondly, it is the normal allophone of /a/ in closed syllables, created by a late rule of the phonology.

    In addition to the forms given in Figure 1, a single initial three-member cluster is attested in the onomatopoetic form <u>tsGe:wtsGews</u> 'bluejay' (D,413). The otherwise exceptionless exclusion of three-member initial clusters is accounted for by the operation of regular rules of cluster reduction and vowel epenthesis, and need not be independently stated as a condition on syllable structure.

Word-final clusters consist of two, three, or four members. Only /t/, /k/ and /s/ may occur as the third or fourth member of a cluster. Moreover, sonorants are restricted to initial position.[2] Some examples are:

Figure 2

a. sonorant - obstruent

wakəmc	'big old coyote'	D,459
celks	'skin'	D,85
ʔewəntk	'full'	D,30
tweqtewqs	'marsh hawk'	D,337
ʔiwtəmpks	'being heavy'	D,36

b. obstruent - obstruent

cawigətk	'crazy person'	D,118
tləqs	'mullet' (sp)	D,409
lo:Ləpks	'believer'	D,340
pəkst	'barking'	D,400
gətbənwəpkst	'arriving in the future'	D,400

Medial clusters are recorded with as many as five members, with sonorants and obstruents occurring freely. The following examples illustrate:

Figure 3

newtGi	'runs down'	D,260
honksdəl	'towards him'	D,106
hemkənktga	'been talking'	D,165
yəwkkni:	'neighbor'	D,466
ʔilqsʔəls	'to put down pl. objects'	D,129
toqlGa	'stops'	D,129

---

2. The sole exceptions to these generalizations are found in the word final clusters /yl/ and /mns/.

?ilqsGe:ni	'graveyard'	D,152
ntoylGa	'crushes down with a round object'	G,56
nəcpga	'burns up completely'	D,71
scəqcqa	'rattles'	D,72
sdikstgi	'wants someone to smell'	G,66
Ga:yəklgi	'comes to search for'	G,59
swəktktis	'looking like inside'	D,43
gənkənktkdəmna	'been repeatedly hunting'	G,60

(2)-(3) illustrate consonant sequences ranging in length up to five. The question immediately arises whether these sequences can be exhaustively assigned to syllables or whether some elements remain unsyllabified. There is good reason to suppose the latter alternative to be correct. If we assumed that all consonants were assigned to syllables, we would be forced to postulate highly complex clusters in Klamath. Such clusters would frequently violate the commonly observed condition that the inherent sonority of segments within the syllable decreases as we proceed outward from the syllable peak to the syllable margin.

The above examples further demonstrate that the four vowels of Klamath, /i e a o/, occur both long and short. We may thus propose, as an initial hypothesis, that the maximal syllable of Klamath consists of the sequence CV^2C where each C stands for a single consonant and V^2 stands for one or two vowels. This gives us syllabifications like the following, in which certain consonants remain extrasyllabic:

Figure 4

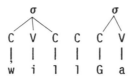

'lies down on the stomach'   G,79

Figure 5

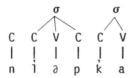

'mashes up with a round object' G,79

We assume that representations containing extrasyllabic segments such as those given in (4)-(5) are well-formed both underlyingly and on the surface. It will be our main purpose in this chapter to motivate this claim.

Barker describes sonorants flanked on both sides by other consonants as "syllabic". He describes these segments as occurring with pitch, but not with stress and, moreover, as not affecting the stress pattern. Furthermore, those segments do not behave as syllable peaks with respect to the syllable sensitive rules of the phonology. Barker's characterization of these segments as "syllabic" should, therefore, be interpreted as a phonetic rather than phonological statement, since these segments fail to meet any of the phonological criteria associated with syllable peaks in Klamath. This analysis is confirmed by the facts of vowel epenthesis in Klamath, to which we now turn.

4.3 Epenthesis

4.3.1 Sonorant Cluster Epenthesis

Consider first the following examples:

Figure 6

a.	tGaləm	'west'	D,406
b.	tGəlməs	'west wind'	D,406
c.	tGaləmdəi̓	'toward the west'	D,406

In (6b) and (6c) we can isolate the suffixes /-as/ and /-dai̓/ which are, respectively, a noun forming and an adjective forming suffix. If we assume a stem of the form /tGalm/, then we see that epenthesis occurs when the stem final consonant is in word final position or followed by a consonant. In terms of the theory developed thus far, the final /m/ is extrasyllabic in our syllable representations in just these two cases. The core syllable structure of all examples in (6) appears in (7):

Figure 7

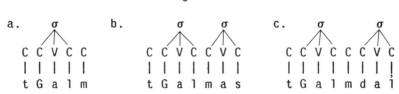

The epenthesis rule in question can be formulated as one that inserts a schwa before a morpheme-final extrasyllabic sonorant consonant, as in (8):

Figure 8

Sonorant Cluster Epenthesis

```
Ø ---> V    / C ___ C' +
        |          |
        ∂        +son
                 +cons
```

This rule applies to the examples in (7) to give, after resyllabification, the structures in (9):

Figure 9

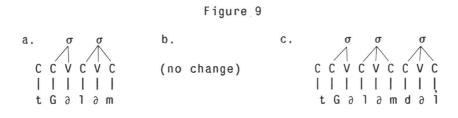

The rule does not apply to (7b) since /m/ is not extrasyllabic.

Unaffiliated sonorants not followed by a morpheme boundary remain unaffected by Sonorant Cluster Epenthesis (8), as the following examples show:

Figure 10

newlGa	/newĺG + a/	'rules'	D,260
Wallwitk	/Wallwi + dk/	'bright-colored'	D,457
sosannGa	/sosannG + a/	'wrestles'	D,383
waGlwis	/waGlw + y + s/	'shinbone awl'	D,430

Further examples were given in (3). This rule also fails to apply to extrasyllabic sonorants in word initial position. This is illustrated by the following examples involving the prefix /n-/ 'act with a round instrument, act upon a round object'.

Figure 11

mboi̯a /n + boí + a/ 'hits in the stomach with a round instrument' D,247

nceq̓a /n + ceq̓ + a/ 'chips with a round instrument'   D,247

nk̓ac̓a /n + k̓ac̓ + a/ 'cuts off the head with a round instrument' D,248

The fact that Sonorant Cluster Epenthesis does not apply to these examples follows from the formulation of our rules. In particular, though the word-initial /n-/ is an extrasyllabic segment occurring morpheme finally, there is no C occurring to its left, as the rule requires.

The rule of Sonorant Cluster Epenthesis provides the first source of confirmation for our analysis of the Klamath syllable. This analysis permits a significant simplification in our formulation of Sonorant Cluster Epenthesis, by allowing it to refer directly to extrasyllabic segments.

4.3.2 General Epenthesis

A second epenthetic process provides further support for our analysis of the syllable. This process, which we term General Epenthesis, applies to certain sequences of four or more consonants, inserting schwa between the second and third of them. The following examples are illustrative.

Figure 12

a.   Gəttk̓a   /Gatdk̓ + a/   'is cold'   D,149
b.   Gətdəks   /Gatdk̓ + s/   'cold' (noun)   D,149
c.   Gətdəkye:ga   /Gatdk̓ + ye:g + a/ 'starts to get cold'   D,149

The suffixes illustrated in these examples are /-a/ (indicative), /-s/ (noun formative) and /-ye:g/ (inceptive). If we take the stem to be /Gatdk̓/, then epenthesis applies just in case a consonant initial suffix follows. Hence in (12b) and (12c), the ə is epenthesized by the following rule, which inserts schwa between two extrasyllabic consonants:

Figure 13

General Epenthesis

Ø ---> V / C' ___ C'
          |
          ə

The underlying trees for the three examples in (12) are:

Figure 14

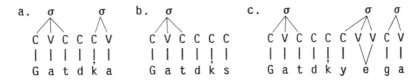

a. σ   σ   b. σ   c. σ   σ   σ
   C V C C C V   C V C C C C   C V C C C C V V C V
   | | | | | | | | | | | | | | | | | | \/ | |
   G a t d k a   G a t d k s   G a t d k y e g a

After the application of (13) and of subsequent resyllabification, (14b-c) are
modified as follows:

Figure 15

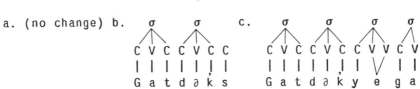

a. (no change) b. σ   σ   c. σ   σ   σ   σ
                  C V C C V C C   C V C C V C C V V C V
                  | | | | | | | | | | | | | | \/ | |
                  G a t d ə k s   G a t d ə k y e g a

Notice that (13) cannot apply to (14a) since neither /t/ nor /k/ are
extrasyllabic. On the other hand, (13) can apply in two different places in
(14b). In order to yield the correct result, as shown in (15b), it is necessary
to restrict the operation of (13) so that it applies directionally from left to
right. Thus, the first application in (14b) triggers resyllabification and the

rule is no longer defined, as the tree in (15b) illustrates.[3]

Before going on to our next epenthetic process, a word about ordering is appropriate. Consider the form [stintgəl]. Underlyingly, this form is composed of /stin/ 'suspend' + /adgl/ 'on the back' and is glossed as follows: /stin + adgl/ 'hangs something on the back'. A rule of Initial Vowel Truncation, to which we return in Chapter 5, deletes the /a/ of /adgl/ and, after resyllabification, the derived tree appears as (16):

Figure 16

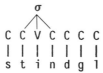

Notice that both epenthesis rules discussed thus far are definable on (16). Notice, however, that Sonorant Cluster Epenthesis applies to introduce an epenthetic /ə/ between /g/ and /l/. Resyllabification will form /gəl/ into a single syllable, thereby bleeding General Epenthesis. If the rules had applied in reverse order, then General Epenthesis would not have bled Sonorant Cluster Epenthesis and a string with two epenthetic vowels would have arisen. Thus, Sonorant Cluster Epenthesis must be ordered before General Epenthesis.

---

3. By independent rules (not formalized here), /k/ is deglottalized and /d/ is devoiced before another obstruent, giving the surface forms in (12).

4.3.3 Affiliation Rules

There are a number of apparent exceptions to General Epenthesis which shed light on the principles of syllabification in Klamath. These exceptions fall into two general types, and are illustrated below.[4]

Figure 17

a.	wlelqbli	/wlelG + ebli/	'arranges again'	D,451
b.	ʔilqsʔəls	/ʔi + elG + s + 'al + s/	'to put down plural objects'	D,129

Figure 18

a.	boqstGa	/bog + s + tga/	'with camas root'	D,405
b.	q̓a pəkstgi	/q̓a pag + sdgi/	'you bark a lot'	D,296
c.	woni:pokksta	/woni:b + 'ok + ksta/	'on all four sides'	D,193
d.	swəktktis	/swa + CC + akt + y + s/	'looking like inside'	D,43

Figure 19

a.	sinamstnank	/sinams + otn + ank/	'having become afraid'	D,366
b.	Nəyksta	/Nay + ksta/	'on one side'	D,272
c.	honksdai̓	/ho + n + g + s + dai̓/	'toward him'	D,106
d.	sdikscna	/sdig + s + cn + a/	'goes along smelling'	D,355

(See also examples given in (3) and (4) earlier.) Examination of these examples shows that they fall under certain subgeneralizations. First, the examples in (17) involve four-member clusters in which the first or final member (or both) is a sonorant. Second, the examples in (18) involve clusters in which C_2 is /s,t,d,k, or g/. The examples in (19) meet both of these conditions. We thus have the following statement:

---

4. Notice that vowel initial morphemes are subject to the early rule of Initial Vowel Truncation, mentioned just above and discussed further in Chapter 5.

Figure 20

General Epenthesis in a sequence C_1C_2 C_3 C_4 is blocked when either:

(i) C_1 or C_4 are sonorants, or

(ii) C_2 is one of the obstruents /s,t,d,k, or g/.

Neither of these conditions is exceptionless. Thus we find epenthesis in examples like the following, where condition (20i) is satisfied:

Figure 21

loykə́tga   /loyk̓ + odg + a/   'been to pick berries'   D,223

ʔitgəbli   /ʔi + odg + ebli/   'takes objects out of a container again'   G, 58

Thus, General Epenthesis in four-member clusters is optional or sporadic when (20i) or (20ii) are met, and otherwise obligatory.[5] There is a straightforward way of treating these apparent exceptions within the present framework. We propose that the epenthesis rules are collectively bled by a set of <u>syllable affiliation</u> rules, which apply to affiliate certain extrasyllabic consonants to adjoining syllables. Thus, one such rule optionally adjoins an extrasyllabic obstruent to the same syllable as an adjoining sonorant. For instance, the examples of (17), following the rule of Initial Vowel Truncation (see footnote 4) and subsequent resyllabification, have the representation given in (22) where the broken lines indicate the operation of the rule in question:

---

5. The suffix /dk/, 'in a state of having been ...ed', is a lexically-marked exception which never undergoes epenthesis. Two homophonous suffixes, /s~as/ 'noun formant' and /s~as/ 'objective' show irregular allomorphy which seems synchronically unrelated to the epenthesis rule. Also, a formative /wal~awl~wl/ 'cover, put on top' shows apparently unpredictable allomorphy. Otherwise this statement seems to have no exceptions. See (25) and following for further discussion of the /s~as/ allomorphy.

Figure 22

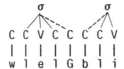 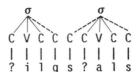

As a consequence of the operation of this affiliation rule, the rule of General Epenthesis is no longer defined.[6]

The affiliation rule that accounts for condition (20ii) has the effect illustrated by the dashed line in (23):

Figure 23

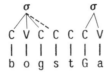 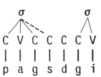

It affiliates an extrasyllabic /s,t,d,k, or g/ to the preceding syllable, regardless of the nature of the preceding consonant. Once again, it has the effect of bleeding the operation of General Epenthesis. We state our affiliation rules as follows:

---

6. We formulate this rule of affiliation as an optional rule under the assumption that the forms in question show free variation depending on whether the epenthetic schwa is present or absent. It is difficult to determine from Barker's description whether this predicted free variation occurs in fact, since Barker's usual (though not invariant) practice is to record just one form of each item. If, in fact, we are not dealing with free variation but with unpredictable lexical allomorphy, then we must allow the presence of syllable-final sonorant + obstruent clusters and syllable-initial obstruent + sonorant clusters as a free option which may or may not be selected in the lexical entry of any Klamath word. Under this alternative, the maximal syllable in Klamath would be defined as $C^2V^2C^2$, where C^2 is the maximal cluster, subject to the condition that it may consist only of a sonorant plus an obstruent (proceeding outward from the vocalic nucleus).

Figure 24

Obstruent Affiliation Rules

a. First Rule   b. Second Rule

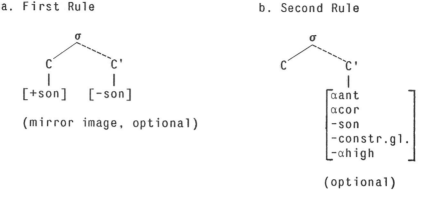

(mirror image, optional)   (optional)

4.3.4 Epenthesis in Final Clusters

The analysis given so far provides a full account of surface consonant clusters in initial and medial position. As we have seen, initial clusters consist of two members only. Each member may be either a sonorant or an obstruent. Thus, the initial cluster types are: OO, OS, SO and SS. In the case of OS clusters obstruent affiliation (24a) may optionally apply, with no consequences for later rules. In the remaining three cases the initial member of the cluster remains extrasyllabic. Neither of our rules of epenthesis are defined upon any of these forms.

Turning to medial clusters, all two-member clusters are of course fully syllabified in core syllable structure. In the case of three-member clusters, Sonorant Cluster Epenthesis (8) is defined only in the case where the medial member of the cluster is both a sonorant and morpheme final. When this sonorant is not morpheme final, the cluster will appear on the surface. Four-member medial clusters have the property that either the first or fourth member is a sonorant, or else the second member is /s,t,d,k, or g/. If an underlying four member cluster does not satisfy either of these constraints, then General Epenthesis (13) operates to break up the cluster. Thus, all of the data illustrated in (1) and (3) are accounted for by the rules given so far.

Given the principles and rules thus far, the constraints on final clusters are automatically accounted for. These clusters, as noted before, comprise two, three or four members. In the case of two member clusters, only obstruent-final clusters are attested; sonorant-final sequences are systematically excluded as a result of Sonorant Cluster Epenthesis (8). Three-member clusters either have a sonorant as their first member, or /s,t,d,k, or g/ as their second member. Furthermore, the final two members are always obstruents. Once again these constraints are predicted by our rules, First Obstruent Affiliation (24a), Second Obstruent Affiliation (24b) and Sonorant Cluster Epenthesis (8), respectively.

A few final four-member clusters are found: /mpks/, /lpks/, /lqst/, /ykst/ (cf. Barker's <u>Grammar</u> p. 48), as well as /pkst/. It will be noted that the principles given so far extend to these clusters as well. In particular, note that such clusters require (24a) to be ordered before (24b), as we have already assumed. Thus, in a final cluster like that of <u>gempks</u> 'the going' (durative), from /ge + en + obg + s/, a four member cluster is created by Initial Vowel Truncation, which deletes the /o/. (24a) applies then, affiliating the /b/, and (24b) applies next, affiliating the /gs/. Finally, /nbgs/ becomes [mpks] by regular rules.[7]

Barker discusses a further set of cases of epenthesis in final clusters which are not covered by the rules given above. Three cases are involved; namely, (a) epenthesis before consonants other than members of the set /s,t,d,k, or g/, and (b) epenthesis before two formatives to which Barker assigns the underlying form /s/ (see Barker, <u>Grammar</u> 60-65 and our

---

7. We assume that (24b) applies to maximal sequences of consonants meeting its description. This assumption is independently needed to account for final clusters like /pkst/ (cf. (2) above). It also accounts for the absence of epenthesis in the five-member cluster of [gənkənktkdəmna] 'been repeatedly hunting', G,60.

footnote 5). These are illustrated in (25a) and (25b), respectively:

Figure 25

a.	tápəq	/tápq/	'leaf'	G,62
	tĭtəq	/tĭtq/	'swallow (bird)'	G,62
b.	kóYəs	/kóY + s/	'louse'	G,60
	s?abəs	/s?ab + s/	'sun'	G,61
	wásəs	/wás + s/	'coyote' (objective)	G,60

The forms in (25a) illustrate the need for an additional, lexically restricted rule inserting schwa before a word final extrasyllabic consonant. The forms in (25b) illustrate epenthesis before the special formatives having the shape /s/. It is noteworthy that this apparent epenthesis applies unpredictably in Barker's data. For example, it does not apply to the following:

Figure 26

sɫəps	/sɫáb + s/	'bloom'	G,61
swəlqs	/swálq + s/	'sweat'	G,62

Since our rule of Second Obstruent Affiliation (24b) applies to these instances of final /s/, no epenthesis rule can apply, and the forms in (26) are regular. Those in (25b), on the other hand, are unexpected. The schwa in these examples cannot be predicted by a regular phonological rule. Rather than postulating a lexically irregular epenthesis rule, we assume that the two suffixes in question have the irregular allomorph /-as/ which is lexically selected by certain stems.[8]

4.3.5 Glide Epenthesis

We now turn to two final rules of epenthesis which confirm the syllable analysis given so far, and which will be of central importance to our subsequent discussion. These are the rules responsible for the vocalization of extrasyllabic glides. Their operation is illustrated by the following forms:

Figure 27

a.	w^{u}boĺa	/w + boĺ + a/	'hits in stomach	D,425
			with long instrument'	
	w^{u}qiwa	/wqiw + a/	'extends out onto a plain'	D,456
	w^{u}q̓əs	/wq̓as/	'quartz'	D,456
b.	tabi:ni	/tabẏ + ni/	'the youngest'	D,401
	delo:ga	/delwg + a/	'attacks'	D,112
	sgoyo:cn̓a	/sgoyw + cn̓ + a/	'sends someone along'	D,362
	mo̓lo:wəpk	/mo̓lw + wabg/	'will be ready'	D,246
	gayo:wi	/ga + aywwi/	'disperse'	D,53
	s?ayo:ga	/s?aywg + a/	'learns'	D,342
c.	tabi:	/tabẏ/	'last'	D,401
	na̓ki:	/na + aḱy/	'close it'	D,46
	?ico:	/?i + acw/	'put grease on someone's hair'	D,42

As these examples show, a glide that is not adjacent to a vowel normally

---

8. Forms like [Glegəpks] 'dead person' G,63 from /Gleg + obg + s/ cannot be accounted for by the epenthesis rules given thus far, since we would have expected the epenthetic schwa before the [k], not the [p], by General Epenthesis. As Barker notes, ə appears before the suffix /-obg/ just in case the preceding morpheme ends in an obstruent or a glottalized or voiceless sonorant. Rather than postulating, as Barker does, a special epenthesis rule applying before this suffix, we propose that this suffix is marked as an exception to Initial Vowel Truncation in the cited context (that is, when an obstruent or a glottalized or voiceless sonorant ends the preceding morpheme). The initial vowel of /-obg/ is changed to schwa by the rule of Vowel Reduction, discussed in the next chapter.

surfaces as a vowel. Moreover, this vowel is long, except in a set of contexts which we discuss in the next chapter. We account for these alternations with the following rules of V-epenthesis. The first applies to word-initial glides and the second to word-internal and word-final glides:

Figure 28

Post-glide Epenthesis

$$\emptyset \;\text{---}> \text{V} \;/\; \text{\#} \; \text{C}' \;\underline{\quad}$$
$$|$$
$$[\text{-cons}]$$

Figure 29

Pre-glide Epenthesis

$$\emptyset \;\text{---}> \text{V} \;/\; \underline{\quad} \; \text{C}'$$
$$|$$
$$[\text{-cons}]$$

The first of these rules inserts a V-element to the right of a word-initial extrasyllabic glide, accounting for the forms in (27a). The second rule inserts a V-element to the left of a word-medial and word-final extrasyllabic glide, accounting for the forms in (27b) and (27c). These rules must be ordered as given. We note that in both cases the [-cons] segment associates with the newly introduced V-element, creating a long vowel. This is an automatic consequence of the Association Conventions given earlier (Chapter 3). The first of these rules has the following effect:

Figure 30

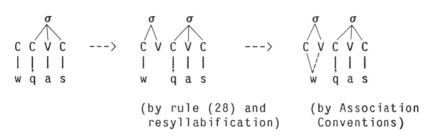

(by rule (28) and   (by Association
resyllabification)   Conventions)

In the resulting configuration, we find the segment [w] attached to the sequence CV on the CV-tier. How is this configuration to be interpreted? It will be recalled that [w] and [u] are nondistinct at the level of the segmental tier, the feature [+syllable] having been eliminated from our feature system. Vowels and their nonsyllabic counterparts are distinguished only by their mode of affiliation to the CV-tier. Accordingly, the segment [w] in the final line of (30) designates a long nonconsonantal segment aligned with two timing units: a syllable-initial C and a following V. This representation is straightforwardly interpreted in terms of the transcription of this sequence given by Barker: [w^u] (Grammar, 28).[9]

Pre-glide Epenthesis (29) is illustrated below:

Figure 31

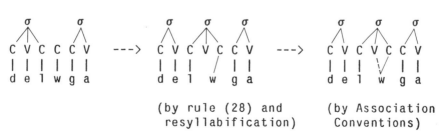

(by rule (28) and   (by Association
resyllabification)   Conventions)

---

9. Here and elsewhere we use the letters w̲ and o̲ interchangeably to designate the same distinctive feature matrix, with the sole difference that o̲ contains the feature [-high], assigned by a late rule.

As we see in this and other examples in (27), a non-initial /w/ dominated by a V-element is realized as [o] by a late lowering rule (see note 9). As will be recalled from Chapter 3, a nonconsonantal segment dominated by the sequence VC on the CV-tier may be interpreted as a long vowel, which together with the lowering rule gives us the correct phonetic output.

It would be appropriate, at this point, to underscore a theoretical assumption underlying the analysis of glides given above; namely, that there are no feature specifications on the CV-tier. By this we mean that CV-elements are not defined in terms of such distinctive feature categories as syllabic or consonantal, but are primitives of the theoretical vocabulary. These elements, as noted earlier, are interpreted as distinguishing the functional category syllable peak from syllable margin and thus determine the locus for the association of prosodic properties such as pitch and stress. In addition, these elements characterize timing units and thus provide the distinction between long and short segments and between simple and complex segments. This account does not entail that any given segment will receive a different articulatory interpretation according to whether it is dominated by a V-element or a C-element on the CV-tier. On the other hand, it does not preclude articulatory features being assigned on the basis of their affiliation to the CV-tier; such features can only be assigned, however, by language particular rules.

Consider, for example, a representation containing the sequence VV dominating the vowel /a/. Compare this with an otherwise identical representation containing the sequence VC dominating the same vowel /a/. What claim does the theory proposed here make with respect to the phonetic realization of these separate representations? That is, is there any necessity to suppose that the /a/ dominated by VV is realized in a given language any differently from an /a/ dominated by VC? The answer is no. In the absence of a language specific rule differentiating these two structures, the theory predicts that they will have identical realizations. A case in point is Turkish (cf. the discussion in 3.4.1 above) in which we found precisely the case under discussion. In this case, it will be recalled, the phonetic realizations were identical.

In the same way, our present analysis of vocalized glides in Klamath characterizes some vowels as being exclusively dominated by V while others (those created by the glide epenthesis rules) as being dominated by the sequence VC. However, as Klamath has no rules differentiating these two types of vowels in terms of quality, they are realized as phonetically identical segments.

To return to our discussion of glide vocalization processes, there is a further process associated with Preglide Epenthesis that requires mention. The introduction of the V-element by this rule automatically triggers the deglottalization or deaspiration of the affected glide, as several of the examples in (27) have already shown. This rule can be stated as follows:

Figure 32

Deglottalization/Deaspiration

$$
\begin{array}{c}
\text{V} \quad \text{C} \\
\diagdown \diagup \\
\text{[-cons]} \; \text{--->} \; \begin{bmatrix} \text{-spread glottis} \\ \text{-constr glottis} \end{bmatrix}
\end{array}
$$

It applies exclusively to the output of Pre-glide Epenthesis (29), with which it can therefore be collapsed.

4.4 Conclusion

In sum, this chapter has demonstrated the role of syllable structure in accounting for a variety of epenthesis rules in Klamath. We have shown that, given a simple account of core syllable representation and two rules of syllable affiliation, we can account for a complex set of epenthesis facts in terms of four epenthesis rules, all of which apply with great generality throughout Klamath word-level phonology.   All of these epenthesis rules make crucial reference in their context to extrasyllabic segments, and have the effect, as we have seen, of allowing these segments to become incorporated into syllable structure.

In the chapter which follows, we show that the principles of syllabification motivated here provide the basis for solving a long-standing problem in Klamath phonology.

Chapter 5: Syllable Theory and Global Rules

5.1 The Problem of Vowel Length in Klamath

One of the standard problems of Klamath phonology concerns the distribution of long and short vowels on the surface. In an important study of this problem, Kisseberth (1973a) pointed out that alternations in vowel length could not be described under the then-accepted assumptions of generative phonology. Kisseberth argued that this phenomenon provided evidence for the need to recognize global conditions on phonological rules. These were conditions that made reference to non-adjacent lines in a derivation, rather than to the immediate input of a given rule.

The problem is the following. The surface long vowels [i:] and [o:] have three sources in Klamath. Some derive from underlying long vowels (1a), some derive from underlying vowel-glide sequences (1b), and some derive from underlying glides alone (1c):

Figure 1

a.	?owi:cna	/?o + owi: + cn + a/	'(long objects) go along in a row'	G,137
b.	sa?i:si	/sa + ?aysi/	'keeps something to oneself'	D,28
c.	delo:ga	/delwga + a/	'attacks'	D,112

Klamath has a vowel shortening rule applying to /i:/ and /o:/ in several contexts, as follows:

Figure 2

$$
\begin{array}{lll}
\text{a.} & V{:}C_0 & \underline{\hspace{2em}} \\
\text{b.} & CC & \underline{\hspace{2em}} \ CC \\
\text{c.} & CC & \underline{\hspace{2em}} \ C_0 \# \\
\end{array}
$$

This rule applies only to the type of long vowel illustrated in (1c); that is, to long vowels deriving from underlying glides alone. It accounts for the alternations between glides, long vowels and short vowels in the following forms:

Figure 3

a. (i)   mbotýa   /mbodý + a/   'wrinkle'   D,236

   (ii)   mbodi:tk   /mbodý + dk/   'wrinkle up'   D,236

   (iii)   mbompditk   /mbo + mbodý + dk/   'wrinkled up'   D,237
                                                         (distr.)

b. (i)   smoqya   /smoqy + a/   'has a mouthful'   D,379

   (ii)   smoqi:tk   /smoqy + dk/   'having a mouthful'   D,379

   (iii)   smosmqitk   /smo + smoqy + dk/   'having a mouthful'   D,379
                                                         (distr.)

c. (i)   keys   /ken + y + s/   'snow'   D,186

   (ii)   sGoci:s   /sGoc + y + s/   'breastbone'   D,364

   (iii)   ce:lis   /ce:l + y + s/   'porcupine'   D,74

   (iv)   soynis   /soyn + y + s/   'race'   D,383

d. (i)   leqya   /le + eqy + a/   'puts a round   D,130
                                                    object in the road'

   (ii)   neqi:s   /ne + eqy + s/   (placename)   D,251

   (iii)   selqibli   /se + le + eqy + ebli/   'drives one's car   D,130
                                                    back onto the road'

e. (i)   ləkwa   /la + akw + a/   'puts a round   D,204
                                                    object across'

   (ii)   ?ako:ca   /?a + akw + cn + a/   'just put a long object   D,45
                                                    across and went on'

   (iii)   sasəlkobli   /sa + sa + la + akw + ebli/   'puts round   D,204
                                                    objects back
                                                    across oneself'
                                                    (distr.)

This rule does not apply to long vowels arising from other sources. See (4a), illustrating long vowels arising from underlying long vowels, and (4b), illustrating long vowels arising from vowel-glide sequences:

Figure 4

a. yə́ydi:s   /ya + yadi: + s/   'spirit stones' (distr.)   D,464

    sciwa:go:la   /sciwa:g + o:l + a/   'takes off a skirt'   D,353

    s?awi:kWi:ya   /s?awi:g + Wi:y + a/   'almost became angry'   D,342

    peclə́qWi:s   /pec + elG + Wi:y + s/   'footprint'   D,299

    bonwo:ts   /bonw + o:t + s/   'something to drink with' D,293

    solwo:lgi   /so + lo + o:lgi/   'gathers a round object'   D,292

b. sdə́sdi:nka   /sda + sdayn + ka/   'little heart' (distr.)   D,354

    pnipno:pca   /pni + pniw + abc + a/   'blow out' (distr.)   D,302

    njonji:lga   /njo + njoy + elg + a/   'are numb' (distr.)   D,266

    snikso:lGa   /sni + ksiw + elG + a/   'makes someone dance'   D,193

(The last three examples involve a rule of Initial Vowel Truncation to be discussed just below.)

In order to deal with these facts, Kisseberth proposed that the Vowel Shortening rule was subject to a global condition making it applicable _only_ to long vowels deriving from underlying glides.[1] This chapter shows that given the syllable-based approach to Klamath phonology motivated in the last chapter, the constraints on Vowel Shortening can be readily stated without recourse to global conditioning.

---

1. This formulation was designed to prevent the rule from applying to the cases in (4a) only, but can easily be extended to the cases in (4b) by limiting Vowel Shortening to long vowels derived from underlying postconsonantal glides.   Notice that the global condition cannot be eliminated by adopting an alternative analysis in which glides vocalize as short vowels and are lengthened by a later rule. Underlying short vowels do not lengthen in the environment where this rule would have to apply (Kisseberth 1973a, 17).

5.2 In Preparation for a Solution

Before turning to a syllable-based account of the facts of vowel shortening, we must first examine a number of separate processes of Klamath phonology which will play a role in our solution. These involve Initial Vowel Truncation, Vowel Reduction and Vowel Deletion. We shall examine evidence showing that these rules apply in a cyclic manner.

5.2.1 Initial Vowel Truncation

Consider the following examples:

Figure 5

wewa	/w + ew + a/	'strikes a long instrument in the water'	D,426
?iwa	/?i + ew + a/	'puts plural objects into water'	D,131
hiwwa	/hiw + ew + a/	'spreads out a blanket in water'	D,131
ˈniqwa	/ˈniq + ew + a/	'puts a hand into water'	D,132

These examples illustrate the formative /ew/ 'in water' in various contexts. The initial vowel of this morpheme appears on the surface only when preceded by no other vowel in the same word. Otherwise, it is deleted. As further examples throughout this study show, there is a very general rule in Klamath deleting short morpheme-initial vowels in noninitial syllables. We state this rule as follows:

Figure 6

Initial Vowel Truncation

$$[\text{-cons}] \; \text{---} \!> \; \emptyset \; / \; VC_0 \; + \; [\rule{1cm}{0.4pt}]_V$$

This rule, as formulated in (6), deletes a nonconsonantal segment in

absolute morpheme-initial position when dominated by V and preceded in
the same word by at least one vowel. Note that the segment in question
must be uniquely and exhaustively dominated by V. This condition is
sufficient to restrict Initial Vowel Truncation to short vowels.

5.2.2 Vowel Deletion

We turn next to two processes of central importance in Klamath
phonology; namely, Vowel Reduction and Vowel Deletion. Vowel Deletion
elides the first vowel of a prefix or stem, provided the vowel occurs in an
open syllable and is preceded by at least one syllable in the word. Vowel
Deletion affects the second member of each of the pairs in the following
examples:

Figure 7

a.	(i)	paga	/pag + a/	'barks'	D,296
	(ii)	pəpga	/pa + pag + a/	'bark' (distr.)	D,296
b.	(i)	ltoqa	/ltoq + a/	'thumps with finger and thumb'	D,225
	(ii)	soltqa	/so + ltoq + a/	'thumps oneself with finger and thumb'	D,225
c.	(i)	wpeqa	/w + peq + a/	'hits in the face with a long instrument'	D,308
	(ii)	coqpqa	/coq + peq + a/	'puts the buttocks in someone's face'	D,308
d.	(i)	lopo:ka	/lo + po:k + a/	'puts warpaint on someone'	D,310
	(ii)	solpo:ka	/so + lo + po:k + a/	'puts warpaint on oneself'	D,310

These examples illustrate a variety of prefixes in Klamath. The distributive
prefix illustrated in (7a) is used typically to describe activities carried out by

several actors. This prefix consists formally of a reduplication of the C_1V sequence that follows it. (7b) illustrates the reflexive/reciprocal prefix /sV-/, where V indicates a copy of the first following vowel. (7c) involves the prefixes /w-/ 'to act with a long instrument' and /coq-/ 'to act with the buttocks'. It will be noted that only the second of these prefixes provides the condition for vowel deletion.   The first prefix in (7dii) is the reflexive/reciprocal prefix /sV-/ seen earlier. As this example shows, prefix vowels as well as root vowels are subject to Vowel Deletion. (We return to the formulation of Vowel Deletion just below.)

5.2.3 Vowel Reduction

We next turn to the rule of Vowel Reduction. If a vowel meets all of the conditions for Vowel Deletion with the exception of the open syllable condition (that is, if the vowel occurs in an initial, closed syllable of a root or prefix and is preceded by at least one syllable), then it undergoes reduction to schwa:

Figure 8

a.	(i)	dmesga	/dmesg + a/	'seizes'	D,119
	(ii)	dedməsga	/de + dmesg + a/	'seize' (distr.)	D,119
b.	(i)	conwa	/conw + a/	'vomits'	D,79
	(ii)	hoscənwa	/hos + conw + a/	'makes vomit'	D,79
c.	(i)	sipca	/sipc + a/	'puts out a fire'	D,366
	(ii)	sisəpca	/si + sipc + a/	'put out a fire' (distr.)	D,366
d.	(i)	Gəttḱa	/Gatdḱ + a/	'is cold'	D,149
	(ii)	GaGəttḱa	/Ga + Gatdḱ + a/	'are cold' (distr.)	D,149

(8a-d) illustrate the application of Vowel Reduction to each of the vowels

/e,o,i,a/.[2]

In addition to the prefixes seen earlier, (8b) involves the causative prefix /hVs/. Notice that Vowel Copy must precede Vowel Reduction in all cases since, otherwise, one would erroneously copy the schwa produced by Vowel Reduction into the reduplicated prefix syllable.

There is evidence from loanwords that both of the processes illustrated in (7) and (8) are fully productive. While Barker does not record any verbs in the loanword vocabulary, he records a small number of nouns borrowed from Chinook and English. Diminutive plurals are formed by suffixing one of the formatives /-ka/ or /-'aːk/ and prefixing the "distributive" formative /C₁V-/. Whenever the conditions for Vowel Deletion or Vowel Reduction are met, they apply, as illustrated in (9):

Figure 9

a.	(i)	poliːs	/poli:+s/	'police'	D,302
	(ii)	popliːka	/po+poli:+ka/	'little policemen' (distr.)	D,302
b.	(i)	pikca	/pikca/	'picture'	D,301
	(ii)	pipǝkca?aːk	/pi+pikca+'aːk/	'little pictures' (distr.)	D,301

The rule of Vowel Deletion can be simply formulated in terms of hierarchical syllable structure. In order to do this we must consider three things: namely, (1) the proper formulation of the rule of Vowel Reduction; (2) the proper formulation of the rule of Vowel Deletion, and (3) their relative order. It will be noticed that if Vowel Reduction is ordered before Vowel Deletion, the formulation of Vowel Reduction will be simplified in that it will not be necessary to state the closed syllable condition in the structural description of the rule: Vowel Reduction can apply in both open and closed

---

2. The schwa in (8di) is not created by Vowel Reduction but by the rule replacing /a/ with schwa in closed syllables (cf. footnote 1, Chapter 4.)

syllables, and subsequently reduced vowels that occur in open syllables can be deleted. This ordering is, moreover, imposed upon us by forms such as the following, which were first noticed in this connection by Thomas (1974):

Figure 10

a.	(i)	nkililka	/nkililk + a/	'is dusty'	D,267
	(ii)	sninklilka	/sni + nkililk + a/	'makes dusty'	D,267
b.	(i)	slowiWya	/slowiWy + a/	'trots'	D,377
	(ii)	hoslwiWya	/hos + slowiWy + a/	'makes trot'	D,377
c.	(i)	cawiga	/cawig + a/	'is crazy'	D,83
	(ii)	snəcwiga	/sna + cawig + a/	'drives someone crazy'	D,83

In each case we are dealing with a bisyllabic root: /nkililk/, /slowiWy/, and /cawig/, respectively. In the first member of each pair, neither Vowel Deletion nor Vowel Reduction apply since no vowel meets the necessary conditions (i.e. no root initial vowel is preceded by at least one syllable). On the other hand, when a prefix is added, the root initial vowel now satisfies the conditions for Vowel Deletion. This is illustrated in the second member of each pair. Notice that if Vowel Deletion were allowed to apply before Vowel Reduction, Vowel Reduction would incorrectly apply to the second vowel:

Figure 11

/sni + nkililk + a/
sni + nklilk + a   Vowel Deletion
*sni + nkləlk + a   Vowel Reduction

Therefore, we must order Vowel Reduction before Vowel Deletion:

Figure 12

/sni + nkililk̓ + a/

sni + nkəlilk̓ + a   Vowel Reduction

sni + nklilk̓ + a   Vowel Deletion

We give the following preliminary formulation of Vowel Reduction:

Figure 13

$$[\text{-cons}] \; \text{---}> \; \partial \;\; / \; VC_0 \; + \; C_0 \; [\text{\_\_\_\_}]_V$$

This formulation makes explicit the fact that Vowel Reduction applies only to the first vowel of a morpheme, provided it is in a noninitial syllable. The rule replaces a [-cons] segment with a schwa provided that it is uniquely and exhaustively dominated by a V element; that is, provided that it is a short vowel. All suffixes are marked as exceptions to Vowel Reduction. We may further observe that under the assumption that this rule is a cyclic rule (see section 5.3.2 for justification), the strict cycle condition predicts that it cannot apply entirely within a single nonderived morpheme. Thus, the internal + boundary in (13) is superfluous and the rule can be reformulated as:

Figure 14

Vowel Reduction

$$[\text{-cons}] \; \text{---}> \; \partial \; / \; VC_0 \; [\text{\_\_\_\_}]_V$$

We now consider the formulation of Vowel Deletion. Assuming that this rule applies to the output of Vowel Reduction, it may be formulated as follows:

Figure 15

Vowel Deletion

$$V \longrightarrow \emptyset \; / \; \underline{\hspace{1.5cm}} \; \sigma$$
$$| $$
$$ \partial $$

This rule states that schwa (together with the V dominating it) is deleted if there is a following sequence in the word that is analyzable as a syllable. This condition is sufficent to guarantee, first, that Vowel Deletion does not apply word finally,[3] and second, that it applies only in open syllables (since schwas in closed syllables will not be immediately followed by a string of segments analyzable as a syllable). We derive [pəpga] (cf. (7a) above) as follows:

Figure 16

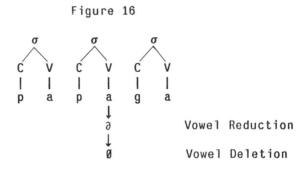

Vowel Reduction

Vowel Deletion

After the operation of Vowel Reduction, the condition for Vowel Deletion is satisfied since there is a sequence of elements immediately following the schwa, namely the sequence /pa/, which is analyzable as a syllable.

---

3. Thus, Vowel Deletion will not apply to the final vowel in words like [psepsə] 'daytime' from /pse + pse/.

Since the only schwas occurring in the input to Vowel Deletion are those created by Vowel Reduction, it is not necessary to repeat the environment of Vowel Reduction in the structural description of Vowel Deletion.   There is considerable evidence in favor of restricting the application of Vowel Deletion in this way. First, Vowel Deletion never affects vowels in the first syllable of a word. This follows in our analysis from the fact that Vowel Reduction never applies in the first syllable of a word. Second, suffixes never undergo Vowel Reduction or Vowel Deletion. Thus, for example, the word-final suffixes /-i/ 'imperative singular', /-ek/ 'l. p. sg. hortatory', /-a/ 'indicative' never appear as schwa, and never delete by Vowel Deletion.   In our analysis, by marking all suffixes as exceptions to Vowel Reduction, we automatically make them ineligible for Vowel Deletion as well.   Third, we have already seen that Vowel Deletion never affects the second syllable of bisyllabic roots: cf. (10c) above. This follows again from our formulation of Vowel Reduction, which can never apply to this syllable. Fourth, let us consider the behavior of two reduplicative formatives which may be prefixed to roots. Under apparently unpredictable conditions, these formatives may block Vowel Reduction in an immediately following morpheme:

Figure 17

a.	(i)	Wiːctgi	/Wiːc + dgi/	'becomes stiff'	D,458
	(ii)	WicWicḷi	/CVC + Wic + ḷi/	'stiff'	D,458
b.	(i)	pétqá	/pétq + a/	'blinks once'	D,308
	(ii)	pétqpetqá	/CVCC + petq + a/	'blinks'	D,308
c.	(i)	céːltgi	/cel' + dgi/	'turns shiny'	D,85
	(ii)	célcel?i	/CVC + cel' + ḷi/	'shining'	D,85

Consequently, the reduplicated forms in (17) must be marked as exceptions to Vowel Reduction. We have just seen, however, that the present system predicts that the failure, for whatever reason, of Vowel Reduction necessarily entails the failure of Vowel Deletion. We now verify this prediction in (18), which displays forms in which both rules fail to apply:

Figure 18

a. (i)   kə́tsga   /kát + osg + a/   'tooth falls out'   D,198

    (ii) kə́tkata   /CVC + kát + a/   'teeth chatter'   D,198

b. (i)   sjíqa   /s + jíq + a/   'prods someone   D,178

                                                 in the ribs'

    (ii) sniji:qjíqa   /sni + CVVC + jíq + a/   'tickles'   D,178

In the second member of pairs (a) and (b) in (18), the penultimate vowel has neither been reduced nor deleted. Thus, our prediction is borne out. Furthermore, Barker notes some interspeaker variation according to whether given roots following the reduplicative formatives illustrated above undergo Vowel Deletion, or neither Vowel Deletion nor Vowel Reduction. Thus, both of the following variants are attested:

Figure 19

dopdópa,   doptpa   /CVC + dop + a/   'boils'   D,122

However, no variants are attested in which a vowel is reduced but not deleted in an open syllable, for example: *[dopdəpa]. Again, these facts follow naturally from our analysis: Vowel Deletion takes place if and only if Vowel Reduction has taken place. In sum, we see that Vowel Reduction and Vowel Deletion share the same set of idiosyncratic restrictions on their applicability. This fact is accounted for in an analysis in which Vowel Deletion applies only to vowels which have been created by the prior application of Vowel Reduction.

5.3 The Cycle in Klamath

We now consider the interaction of Pre-glide Epenthesis, discussed in Chapter 4, and Vowel Deletion. Consider forms such as the following:

Figure 20

a.	i.	swina	/swin + a/	'sings'	D,398
	ii.	swiso:nis	/swi + swin + y + s/	'singer'	D,398
b.	i.	tweqa	/twe + eqn + a/	'bore through'	D,414
	ii.	teto:qa	/te + twe + eqn + a/	'bore through' (distr.)	D,414
c.	i.	swicɔqcq̓a	/swi + CVC + ciq̓ + a/	'shake the head'	D,398
	ii.	swiso:cɔqcq̓a	/swi + swi + CVC + ciq̓ + a/	'shake the head' (distr.)	D,398
d.	i.	swapɔtta	/swa + pat + otn + a/	'tie to a tree'	D,396
	ii.	swaso:pɔtta	/swa + swa + pat + otn + a/	'tie to a tree' (distr.)	D,396

To derive (20aii), our rules must apply as follows:

Figure 21

/swi + swin + y + s/

swi + swin + i: + s	Pre-glide Epenthesis
swi + swɔn + i: + s	Vowel Reduction
swi + swn + i: + s	Vowel Deletion
swi + so:n + i: + s	Pre-glide Epenthesis
swi + so:n + i + s	Vowel Shortening (see below)

Pre-glide Epenthesis must be able to precede Vowel Deletion, which it feeds by creating an open syllable environment. On the other hand, Pre-glide Epenthesis must be able to reapply after Vowel Deletion, which feeds it.

We propose, following, in particular, Kisseberth (1973b), that some rules of Klamath, including Pre-glide Epenthesis, Vowel Reduction, and Vowel Deletion, are cyclic rules. We take Klamath words to have right-branching structures in which each prefix (that is, members of Barker's verb prefix classes 1-6 and noun prefix classes 1-2) constitutes a new cycle. On this assumption the output of each cycle may, in principle, be an independent lexical entry. Now Pre-glide Epenthesis, Vowel Reduction and Vowel Deletion interact properly, with Vowel Deletion ordered before Pre-glide Epenthesis:

Figure 22

	[swi [+ swin + y + s]]	Underlying Representation
1st cycle:	swin + iː + s	Pre-glide Epenthesis
2nd cycle:	swi + swən + iː + s	Vowel Reduction
	swi + swn + iː + s	Vowel Deletion
	swi + soːn + iː + s	Pre-glide Epenthesis
	swi + soːn + i + s	Vowel Shortening (see below)

The need to recognize the cyclic organization of segmental rules in Klamath has been questioned in other work, including White (1973), Thomas (1974) and Feinstein and Vago (1981). However, these writers have not, in our opinion, provided convincing alternatives to cyclic rule analyses. In this section and in Section 5.3.1 we review the evidence supporting the recognition of a segmental cycle in Klamath, and in Section 5.3.2 we examine the relevance of the Klamath evidence for the principle of the strict cycle. In a final section of this chapter, Section 5.5, we examine the reanalysis of the Klamath data proposed in the most recent of these studies, Feinstein and Vago (1981), and show that it cannot account for the full range of data discussed in this study.

Before continuing, we note that the Resyllabification Convention (see Chapter 2) is crucial to the derivation given in (22). Notice, in particular, that after the operation of Vowel Deletion on cycle 2, the resulting structure is resyllabified, yielding:

Figure 23

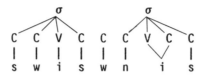

The medial /w/ is extrasyllabic, since as a sonorant it does not satisfy the conditions for syllabification. At this point, Pre-glide Epenthesis applies. The resulting structure is resyllabified once again, and the following structure is created:

Figure 24

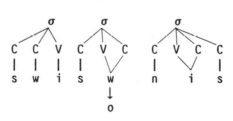

We have given evidence, then, that there is at least one derivation in Klamath in which Pre-glide Epenthesis must apply twice, once before Vowel Deletion and once after Vowel Deletion. This conclusion depends upon our assumption that the noun-forming suffix given by Barker as /y/ is, in fact, an underlying glide, rather than a vowel. The motivation for this analysis is that this formative occurs with three alternants: [y], [i] and [i:], as illustrated earlier (cf. (3c) above).[4] The first of these alternants occurs when /y/ is adjacent to a vowel, the second under the conditions defining Vowel Shortening (2), and the third in all remaining environments. This is the alternation pattern characteristic of underlying glides; as we noted at the outset, underlying vowels do not show analogous length alternations. Following Barker's analysis, then, we take the existence of [y]~[i]~[iː] and [w]~[o]~[oː] alternations as establishing sufficient conditions for a glide analysis.[5]

However, evidence for the cyclic application of Pre-glide Epenthesis is not limited to forms containing the noun formative /y/. We shall take the form [swisoːnis] and the other forms in (20) as establishing, in any case, the need to allow Pre-glide Epenthesis to apply after Vowel Deletion, and turn now to further evidence for the application of Pre-glide Epenthesis before Vowel Deletion. This evidence is given in (25).

Figure 25

a. (i) qbə́tya   /qbaty + a/   'wraps the legs around' D,315
   (ii) qbəqptiːwəpk /qba + qbaty + wabg/ 'will wrap their legs   D,315
                                          around' (distr.)
b. (i) smóqya   /smoqy + a/   'has a mouthful'   D,379
   (ii) smósmqitk   /smo + smoqy + dk/   'having a mouthful'   D,379
c. (i) sponiː   /spon + oy/   'gives someone'   D,387
   (ii) spospni   /spo + spon + oy/   'give a person' (distr.)   D,387

Here we are dealing with the roots /qbaty/ 'wrap the legs around', /smoqy/ 'have a mouthful' and /spon/ 'guide', and the suffix /-oy/ 'give', among others. Note that Initial Vowel Truncation applies to the forms of (25c),

---

4. See Kisseberth (1973b) and Barker (1963) for further examples.
5. White's attempt (1973) to reanalyze the noun-forming suffix as /iː/ required the introduction of an extremely ad hoc set of assumptions in order to account for the length facts. See Thomas (1974) for critical discussion.

feeding Pre-glide Epenthesis. What is of interest in all of these forms is the fact that Vowel Deletion applies to the initial root vowel in the second member of each pair in all cases, even though this vowel is followed by two or more non-syllabic segments in the rule's input. The explanation here is simple. Assuming that Vowel Reduction and Vowel Deletion are cyclic rules, the correct interaction between Pre-glide Epenthesis and Vowel Deletion follows automatically. Thus, for example, on the initial stem cycle of (25aii), where we encounter [qbaty + wabg], Pre-glide Epenthesis is applicable, changing [y] to [iː].[6] On the second (word-level) cycle, where we encounter [qba + qbati: + wabg], both Vowel Reduction and Vowel Deletion are defined, eliminating the second [a]. What is crucial here is that the operation of Pre-glide Epenthesis on the previous cycle will place the schwa resulting from Vowel Reduction in an open syllable, making it eligible for Vowel Deletion. A similar account holds for the remaining examples.

A noncyclic account of these rules is unable to provide a satisfactory account of the relation between Vowel Deletion, Pre-glide Epenthesis, and syllable structure. Consider, for example, an alternative, noncyclic analysis in which a separate case of Vowel Deletion is introduced to delete schwa before the consonant-glide sequence:

Figure 26

Vowel Deletion (reformulation)

$$
\begin{matrix} V \\ | \\ \partial \end{matrix}
\;\;\text{---}\!\!>\;\; \emptyset \;/\;
\left\{
\begin{matrix}
\underline{}\; \sigma \\[4pt]
\underline{}\; C\;[\text{-cons}]
\end{matrix}
\right\}
$$

This formulation would permit a noncyclic derivation of the examples under

---

6. Recall that /wabg/, as a suffix, is marked [-Vowel Reduction]. Its vowel will be converted to schwa by the late rule referred to in footnote 2.

consideration:

Figure 27

/swi + swin + y + s/	/qba + qbaty + wabg/	
swi + swən + y + s	qba + qbaty + wabg	Vowel Reduction
swi + swn + y + s	qba + qbty + wabg	Vowel Deletion (26)
swi + so:n + i: + s	qba + qbti: + wabg	Pre-Glide Epenthesis
swiso:nis	qbaqpti:wapk	(later rules)

The problem, however, is that the revised rule deletes schwas too generally before consonant-glide sequences. The following examples show that Vowel Deletion does not take place in case the consonant-glide sequence is itself followed by either a vowel (28a,b) or a non-prevocalic glide (28c,d):

Figure 28

a. (i) conwa   /conw + a/   'vomits'   D,79

   (ii) cocənwa   /co + conw + a/   'vomit' (distr.)   D,79

b. (i) swelwa   /swelw + a/   'tangles up'   D,399

   (ii) sweswəlwa   /swe + swelw + a/   'tangle up' (distr.)   D,399

c. (i) wenwitk   /wenwy' + dk/   'widow'   D,440

   (ii) wewənwitk   /we + wenwy' + dk/   'widows' (distr.)   D,440

d. (i) qbaqa   /qbaq + a/   'braids someone's   D,315

                                              hair'

   (ii) səqbəqwis   /sa + qbaq + w + y + s/ 'a single braid'   D,315

Thus, to account for further examples like these, the revised Vowel Deletion Rule would have to be the following:

Figure 29

Vowel Deletion (second reformulation)

$$
\begin{array}{ll}
V \quad ---> \emptyset \ / \quad
\left\{
\begin{array}{l}
\underline{\quad}\sigma \\[2ex]
\underline{\quad} \ C \ [-cons] \ \left\{
\begin{array}{l}
[-cons] \ V \\
[+cons] \\
\#\#
\end{array}
\right\}
\end{array}
\right\}
&
\begin{array}{l}
\text{a.} \\[3ex]
\text{b.} \\
\text{c.} \\
\text{d.}
\end{array}
\end{array}
$$

This version of the rule replaces the second case of (26) with three new cases, (29b-d). The first, (29b), is required for examples like (25a). It allows Vowel Deletion to take place before a consonant-glide sequence followed by another glide which is in turn followed by a vowel. The second, (29c), allows the consonant-glide sequence to be followed by a true consonant, and accounts for examples like (25b). The third case, (29d), allows the consonant-glide sequence to be word-final, and accounts for examples like (25c).

One problem with this reformulation of the rule is that it is complex and arbitrary, applying in four formally distinct environments. It is possible to collapse the four cases of (29) into one rule only if the open syllable condition expressed by the first case is "translated" into an expression not making reference to the σ-tier. This would permit the following, final formulation:

Figure 30

$$
\begin{array}{l}
V \ ---> \emptyset \ / \ \underline{\quad\quad\quad} \ C \ <C>_a \quad << C < V >_d>_b \ X \ >_e \ \#\# \\[1ex]
\quad | \qquad\qquad\qquad\quad\ | \qquad\qquad | \\[1ex]
\quad \partial \qquad\qquad\qquad [-cons] \ <[-cons]>_c
\end{array}
$$

$$
\begin{array}{ll}
\text{condition:} & a \ ---> \ b \ \text{or not} \ e \\
& c \ ---> \ d
\end{array}
$$

The main problem with a noncyclic analysis incorporating this rule (or the descriptively equivalent prior formulation in (29)) is not sheer complexity, however. It is the fact that it fails to express a linguistically significant generalization. Under this analysis, it is mere coincidence that any glide satisfying the first [-cons] segment of the context in (30) (that is, the second term to the right of the dash) also satisfies the conditions for Pre-glide Epenthesis.[7] In other words, this solution is unable to express the fact that the principles of syllabification required to account for Vowel Deletion are identical to those required to account for Pre-Glide Epenthesis. In terms of a noncyclic analysis of Klamath, the only way to incorporate this generalization would be to retain the earlier formulation of Vowel Deletion given in (26), and place a global condition upon the rule to the effect that a glide in an input string only satisfies the second term to the right of the dash if it later undergoes Pre-glide Epenthesis (cf. derivation (27)). In view of this theoretically undesirable consequence, we maintain that the noncyclic analysis of Klamath must be abandoned. We conclude that (at least) Vowel Reduction, Vowel Deletion as stated in (15) and Pre-glide Epenthesis are cyclic rules in Klamath phonology.

5.3.1 Further Evidence for the Cycle in Klamath

In view of the controversial status of the cycle in segmental phonology, we now consider, more briefly, further cases of rule interaction that show that a subset of rules of Klamath must apply cyclically.

---

7. It must be assumed that Pre-Glide Epenthesis applies from right-to-left, to account for the fact that in a sequence of two non-identical extrasyllabic glides, only the second undergoes the rule.

Our first case involves the interaction of Vowel Reduction and Vowel Deletion with a rule of Glottal Lengthening, first cited as evidence for cyclicity by Kisseberth (1973b). Glottal Lengthening is a rule whereby a glottal stop is deleted preconsonantally and prepausally, and a preceding vowel (if there should be one) is lengthened. The postvocalic environment is illustrated by the following forms, all involving the root morpheme /sle?/ 'see':

Figure 31

sle?a	/sle? + a/	'sees'	D,373
sle:ca	/sle? + ca + a/	'goes to see'	D,374
sle:na	/sle? + na/	'let's see!'	D,374
hesle:	/hes + sle?/	'show!'	D,373
hesle:Wi:ya	/hes + sle? + Wi:y + a/	'almost showed'	D,374

The fact that this rule applies just to glottal stops which occur preconsonantally and prepausally suggests that we are dealing with a syllable-conditioned rule which applies to tautosyllabic vowel-glottal stop sequences. We state it as follows:

Figure 32

Glottal Lengthening

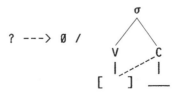

We thus have derivations like the following:

Figure 33

The nature of the interaction between Vowel Reduction, Vowel Deletion, and Glottal Lengthening is shown by forms like the following:

Figure 34

a. ?oyo:qa   /?o + yo:q + a/   'shaves someone'   D,472
b. so:yo:qa   /so + ?o + yo:q + a/   'shaves oneself'   D,473
c. soso:yo:qa   /so + so + ?o + yo:q + a/ 'shave themselves' D,473
                                          (distr.)

The derivation of so:yo:qa (34b) proceeds as follows:

Figure 35

[so [+ ?o [+ yo:q + a]]]
so + ?ə + yo:q + a   Vowel Reduction
so + ? + yo:q + a   Vowel Deletion
so: + yo:q + a   Glottal Lengthening

The derivation of this form is the same whether these rules apply cyclically or not, since under a cyclic analysis these rules are not defined until the outermost prefix cycle. Crucially, however, Vowel Deletion must precede Glottal Lengthening in order for the latter to apply.

To see that Glottal Lengthening is a cyclic rule, we observe that it must bleed the operation of Vowel Reduction on the final cycle of the derivation of soso:yo:q̇a (34c). This result can be achieved if we assume that all three rules are cyclic and that they are ordered as assumed in (35): Vowel Reduction, Vowel Deletion, Glottal Lengthening. The derivation proceeds as in (35) until the end of the next-to-last cycle and then continues as follows:

Figure 36

so + [so: + yo:q̇ + a]	(output of third cycle)
n/a	Vowel Reduction
n/a	Vowel Deletion
n/a	Glottal Lengthening
soso:yo:q̇a	output

In a noncyclic derivation, Vowel Reduction would apply not only to the third prefix /ʔo-/ of (34c), but to the second prefix /so-/ as well, yielding the incorrect form *sosə:ya:q̇a:

Figure 37

/so + so + ʔo + yo:q̇ + a/	Underlying Representation
so + sə + ʔə + yo:q̇ + a	Vowel Reduction
so + sə + ʔ + ya:q̇ + a	Vowel Deletion
so + sə: + yo:q̇ + a	Glottal Lengthening

Vowel Reduction first applies to the second and third prefix vowels. Vowel Deletion, applying (as must be independently assumed) from right to left, deletes the second schwa. Subsequently, Glottal Lengthening applies, yielding the incorrect form. There is no way to prevent this result in a noncyclic derivation.

Further evidence for cyclicity in Klamath comes from a rule which deletes /n/, as follows:

Figure 38

n-Deletion

n ---> Ø / C ___ + a #

This rule applies wherever it is defined and is exceptionless in the data presented by Barker, as far as we have been able to tell. Let us examine the following forms:

Figure 39

a. (i)	yeba	/yebn + a/	'digs'	D,468
(ii)	yeyba	/ye + yebn + a/	'dig' (distr.)	D,468
(iii) cf.	yebno:la	/yebn + o:l + a/	'finishes digging'	D,468
b. (i)	kena	/ken + a/	'snows'	D,185
(ii)	sneka	/sne + ken + a/	'makes it snow'	D,185
c. (i)	swina	/swin + a/	'sings'	D,398
(ii)	swiswa	/swi + swin + a/	'sings' (distr.)	D,398
d. (i)	sge?a	/sge?n + a/	'buys'	D,361
(ii)	hesk?a	/hes + sge?n + a/	'buy from each other'	D,361
(iii) cf.	sge:nənk	/sge?n + ank/	'having bought'	D,361

The example in (39aii) show that n-deletion feeds and thus must precede Vowel Deletion; the examples in (39b,c) show that it is fed by and thus must follow Vowel Deletion; the examples in (39d) show further that it bleeds and thus must precede Glottal Lengthening, which we have already shown to be cyclic. Our derivations follow:

Figure 40

	[ye [+ yebn + a]]	[sne [+ ken + a]]	[hes [+ sge?n + a]]	
1st cycle:	n/a	n/a	n/a	VR
	n/a	n/a	n/a	VD
	yeb + a	n/a	sge? + a	n-Del.
2nd cycle:	ye + yəb + a	sne + kən + a	hes + sgə? + a	VR
	ye + yb + a	sne + kn + a	hes + sg? + a	VD
	n/a	sne + k + a	n/a	n-Del.
	n/a	n/a	hesk?a	other
				rules

We know of no noncyclic account of these and similar forms. Hence, we conclude that n-deletion is in the cycle, ordered after Vowel Reduction and Vowel Deletion but before Glottal Lengthening.

We have offered three independent arguments for the view that at least a subset of the phonological rules of Klamath must apply cyclically. We assume, following current accounts of the phonological cycle, that the cyclic rules form a block preceding a (possibly empty) set of noncyclic (or postcyclic) rules. It follows from this that any rule that can be shown to feed a cyclic rule must itself be a cyclic rule. Thus, for example, Sonorant Cluster Epenthesis, seen earlier, must be a cyclic rule since it crucially feeds Vowel Deletion. To see this, consider the following examples:

Figure 41

a. (i)	debəlsga	/debl + osg + a/	'drops'	D,111
(ii)	detbəlsga	/de + debl + osg + a/	'drop' (distr.)	D,111
b. (i)	sdipəllGa	/sdipn + eĺG + a/	'turns upside down'	D,357
(ii)	sdistpəllGa	/sdi + sdipn + eĺG + a/	'turn upside down' (distr.)	D,357
c. (i)	dilənne:ga	/diln + one:g + a/	'rolls into a hole'	D,115

(ii) sdisdlənne:ga /sdi + s + diln + one:g + a/ 'rolls (distr.)   D,115

into a hole'

In the second member of each pair, it must be assumed that Sonorant Cluster Epenthesis applies before Vowel Deletion, feeding it. Hence, Sonorant Cluster Epenthesis is a cyclic rule. We derive (41bii) as follows:

Figure 42

	[sdi [+ sdipn + eíG + a]]	Underlying representation
1st cycle:	sdipn + íG + a	Initial Vowel Truncation
	sdipən + íG + a	Sonorant Cluster Epenthesis
	n/a	Vowel Reduction
	n/a	Vowel Deletion
2nd cycle:	n/a	Sonorant Cluster Epenthesis
	sdi + sdəpən + íG + a	Vowel Reduction
	sdi + sdpən + íG + a	Vowel Deletion
	sdistpəllGa	other rules

Finally, as further proof that Sonorant Cluster Epenthesis is ordered in the cycle, consider the following forms, all containing the root /sge?n/ 'buy':

Figure 43

sge?a	/sge?n + a/	'buys'	D,361
sge?əmbli	/sge?n + ebli/	'buys back'	D,361
sge:nət	/sge?n + at/	'(plural) buy!'	D,361
sge:ni:ya	/sge?n + i:y + a/	'buys for someone'	D,361
sge:ys	/sge?n + y + s/	'the buying'	D,361

Crucially, Sonorant Cluster Epenthesis applies before Glottal Lengthening, bleeding the latter in [sge?əmbli]; hence Sonorant Cluster Epenthesis is cyclic:

Figure 44

/sge?n + ebli/	Underlying Representation
sge?n + bli	Initial Vowel Truncation
sge?ən + bli	Sonorant Cluster
n/a	Glottal Lengthening

We then have, among others, the following ordered rules, all of which must be placed in the cycle:

Figure 45

Initial Vowel Truncation	(6)
Sonorant Cluster Epenthesis	(8, Chapter 4)
Vowel Reduction	(14)
Vowel Deletion	(15)
Pre-glide Epenthesis	(29, Chapter 4)
n-Deletion	(38)
Glottal Lengthening	(32)

5.3.2 Klamath and the Strict Cycle

As noted earlier in connection with our revised formulation of Vowel Reduction (14), cyclic rule application is usually understood to be subject to a condition of strict cyclicity. One version of this condition, due to Mascaró (1976), reads as follows (we simplify in ways irrelevant to the present discussion):

Figure 46

Cyclic rules apply only to derived representations, where a representation R is derived with respect to a rule S on cycle j iff R meets the structural analysis of S by virtue of:

(i) a combination of morphemes introduced in cycle j,

or

(ii) the previous application of a phonological rule in cycle j.

Alternative versions of this principle, differing only slightly in their empirical predictions, are given in Halle (1978).

The strict cyclicity condition has the effect of accommodating a class of surface exceptions to cyclic rules; namely, those forms which meet the structural description of a cyclic rule but which satisfy neither of the conditions stated in (46). This will be the case when the structural description of a rule is exhaustively satisfied by the underlying representation of a single morpheme; in this case, the rule will not apply. It was because of this condition that we were able to simplify our formulation of Vowel Reduction, stating it as (14), given below for reference:

Figure 47

$$[\text{-cons}] \dashrightarrow \partial \ / \ V \ C_0 \ [\underline{\quad}]_V$$

Under the strict cyclicity condition, this rule will not apply on the innermost cycle to the second stem vowel in forms like [sni [+ nkililk̓ + a]], since the second stem vowel, although otherwise satisfying the rule, occurs in a nonderived representation. Hence, Vowel Reduction will apply only on the second cycle, giving the intermediate form [sni [+ nkəlilk̓ + a]], which then undergoes Vowel Deletion to become the surface form [sninklilk̓a].

While the strict cyclicity condition allows a significant simplification of the statement of Vowel Reduction, there is a class of exceptions to this principle in Klamath to which we now turn. One type of exception is illustrated by the following forms, involving Pre-glide Epenthesis and Glottal Lengthening, respectively:

Figure 48

| a. | delo:ga | /delwg + a/ | 'attacks' (cf. (1)) |
| b. | sge:nət | /sge?n + at/ | 'plural buy!' (cf. (43)) |

These forms, by our assumptions, consist of a single cycle only. The rules of Pre-glide Epenthesis and Glottal Lengthening, which we have earlier shown to be cyclic, apply on this cycle but they do so on what appears to be a nonderived representation, since the rules in question are satisfied by the first morpheme alone. As a further example, consider:

Figure 49

a.	(i)	wibəl	/wibl/	'alder'	D,444
	(ii)	wibləm	/wibl + m/	'alder tree'	D,445
b.	(i)	tGaləm	/tGalm/	'west'	D,406
	(ii)	cf. tGəlməs	/tGalm + as/	'west wind'	D,406

In the first member of each pair, the cyclic rule of Sonorant Cluster Epenthesis has applied on the inner (and only) cycle, in apparent violation of strict cyclicity.

If we compare Vowel Reduction (a rule which obeys the strict cycle) with Pre-glide Epenthesis, Glottal Lengthening and Sonorant Cluster Epenthesis (rules which do not), we notice an important difference betwen them; the latter rules, but not the former, make crucial reference to information involving syllabification and the σ-tier. Thus Glottal Lengthening applies only to tautosyllabic sequences, while Pre-glide Epenthesis and

Sonorant Cluster Epenthesis applies only in the context of extrasyllabic sonorants. We may thus formulate the following additional condition to the strict cycle principle:[8]

Figure 50

Syllable structure creates a derived representation with respect to all rules that refer crucially to it.

5.4 The solution to Vowel Shortening

With this background we may return to the problem stated at the beginning of the chapter. As the reader will recall, Klamath has a rule of Vowel Shortening which applies only to those long vowels that derive from underlying glides (specifically, from underlying glides preceded by a consonant). Long vowels having other sources are not affected by this rule. The rule may be informally stated as follows:

---

8. As it stands, this is merely an ad hoc extension to the strict cycle condition, intended to incorporate a new class of exceptions to it. Kiparsky (1982) points out that given a particular formulation of the Elsewhere Condition, strict cyclicity follows from it as a theorem and need not be stipulated. Kiparsky's proposal is to allow the Elsewhere Condition (appropriately formulated) to apply in the lexicon as well as in the phonology. Assuming (as is required for independent reasons in Kiparsky's approach) that every lexical entry constitutes an identity rule whose structural description is the same as its structural change, the fact that the stem of [sni [+ nkililk + a]] does not undergo Vowel Reduction follows from the fact that the root [nkililk], as a lexical rule, properly includes the structural description of Vowel Reduction under the Elsewhere Condition, and is thus disjunctively ordered with respect to it. What is particularly interesting for the present discussion is that syllable structure, which is assigned cyclically in Kiparsky's framework, automatically "exempts" syllabified forms from the effect of the Elsewhere Condition with respect to rules that refer crucially to syllabification, by creating a derived representation. While we have not attempted to formulate our analysis of Klamath in terms of Kiparsky's framework, it seems to us that further research in this direction might prove fruitful.

Figure 51

A long vowel is shortened in the following environments, provided it is derived from an underlying postconsonantal glide:

a. $V:C_0$ _____
b. CC _____ CC
c. CC _____ C_0 #

We now consider the status of the global condition on this rule.

As many phonologists have pointed out (including Kenstowicz and Kisseberth (1977, 296)), global conditions on rules are extremely powerful devices. The reasons for thinking this are obvious. Accompanying any phonological rule making use of global conditions must be devices which track segments across derivations up to the point of potential application of the rule and from that point on as well. The complexity of such devices is obvious. They require, among other things, that every phonological rule must have available to it a complete derivational history for each segment of each string to which it might apply. This follows since, at any given point in a derivation, there is no way of knowing whether the next rule makes use of a global condition or not. The problems that such theoretical devices pose for processing seem excessive. All other things being equal, it is desirable to eliminate such complexity.[9]

---

9. Kiparsky (1973) also noted the excessive power of global conditions on rules and sought to eliminate them in favor of a principle of cross-linguistic validity which required certain types of rules to apply only in what he described as derived environments. It should be noted that Kiparsky's proposal, while eliminating global conditions on language particular rules, did not eliminate the need for global tracking devices which followed the individual history of segments across derivations. Kiparsky's proposal was subsumed under the elaboration of the notion of strict cycle mentioned in footnote 8 above.

In the face of proposals to eliminate global conditions and despite a consensus among phonological theorists to the effect that global conditions are undesirable, the Klamath data has remained intractable. The value of Kisseberth's observations lies in their demonstration that standard accounts of generative phonology were unable to provide a satisfactory account of shortening in Klamath. Subsequent proposed revisions of Kisseberth's account of Klamath have not offered a solution to this problem and have, for the most part, ignored it. Nonetheless, the facts are clear and well documented and a satisfactory solution to them constitutes, in our view, a condition of adequacy for any account of Klamath phonology. It is for this reason that we turn now to a solution to this problem in terms of the syllable-based theory described above.

Given the analysis developed so far, the solution is trivially simple. Consider first the distinction between underlying long vowels and long vowels created by Pre-glide Epenthesis (cf. (4a) and (3) respectively, given earlier). Underlying long vowels, by our earlier hypothesis, are single units of the segmental tier linked to two consecutive V-elements on the CV-tier. Long vowels derived by Pre-glide Epenthesis, on the other hand, are dominated by the sequence VC on the CV-tier. Thus, in derived structure, these two types of long vowels are formally distinct:

Figure 52

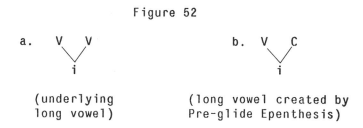

a.   V   V   b.   V   C
       \ /   \ /
        i   i

(underlying   (long vowel created by
long vowel)   Pre-glide Epenthesis)

In the theory of phonology assumed here, shortening rules have the effect of deleting V or C elements. In the present case, we need only assume that

Vowel Shortening has the following form to insure that it will not apply to underlying long vowels of type (52a):

Figure 53

Vowel Shortening

C ---> Ø /   V ____

$$\underset{[\quad]}{\bigvee}$$

(in the environments listed in (51) above)

This rule, then, correctly applies to long vowels derived by Pre-glide Epenthesis while not affecting underlying long vowels.

We have been able to arrive at this solution without the use of global conditions due to the fact that, in our analysis, Pre-glide Epenthesis is not a rule of absolute neutralization. Thus, the output of Pre-glide Epenthesis does not create long vowel representations that are identical to any found in its input. As a result, subsequent rules are able to distinguish between underlying and derived long vowels. This solution exploits the formal possibility of distinguishing between two types of long vowels which are phonetically equivalent: those dominated by VV and those dominated by VC. Earlier chapters have shown that this distinction is independently required in the phonologies of other languages. Indeed, we have shown that at least one other language, Turkish, must be regarded as having long vowels of both types.

To complete our solution, we must consider the second type of surface exception to Vowel Shortening, which consists of those long vowels arising from underlying vowel-glide sequences (cf. (4b) above). Representative examples are repeated here for the reader's convenience (cf. Kisseberth (1973a) for further examples):

Figure 54

sdǝsdi:nka	/sda + sdayn + ka/	'little heart' (distr.)	D,354
pnipno:pca	/pni + pniw + abc + a/	'blow out' (distr.)	D,302
njonji:lga	/njo + njoy + elg + a/	'are numb' (distr.)	D,266
sniksо:lGa	/sni + ksiw + elG + a/	'makes someone dance'	D,193

We observe that an underlying vowel is deleted in all examples, and the following glide appears as the corresponding long vowel. Vowel Deletion as currently formulated cannot account for the deletion of the vowels since Vowel Deletion is restricted to open syllables. Nevertheless, we might consider whether Vowel Deletion should be generalized to account for these forms.

This, in fact, is the approach followed by Kenstowicz and Kisseberth in a solution involving a further global condition (1977, 221-5). They propose that Vowel Deletion be reformulated as a "look ahead" rule, making global reference to the surface level of representation. They propose the following statement:[10]

Figure 55

Vowel Deletion (global version)

$$\partial \dashrightarrow \varnothing$$

Condition: the immediately following consonant does not appear in the ultimate phonetic representation followed by another consonant.

---

10. We have replaced the vowel /a/ in Kenstowicz and Kisseberth's formulation with the vowel /∂/, in conformity with our earlier analysis. This modification has no bearing upon the discussion which follows.

Notice that the forms in (54) meet this condition if one takes "appear" to mean "appear unaltered". This seems to be the sense intended by Kenstowicz and Kisseberth, and we give this interpretation to the condition in the following discussion. We derive the form "little heart" by way of illustration:

Figure 56

/sda + sdayn + ḱa/
 sda + sdəyn + ḱa   Vowel Reduction
 sda + sdyn + ḱa   Vowel Deletion (global version)
 sda + sdi:n + ḱa   Pre-glide Epenthesis
 sdəsdi:nḱa   other rules

In this derivation Vowel Reduction applies on the second cycle, as in our analysis. Subsequently, the global version of Vowel Deletion (55) applies, followed by Pre-glide Epenthesis and the late rule creating schwa from /a/ in closed syllables. Note that the application of Vowel Deletion is legitimate here because the global condition is satisfied: the consonant following the deleted vowel does not appear unaltered in the ultimate phonetic representation. We see, then, that the effect of reformulating Vowel Deletion as Kenstowicz and Kisseberth have done is to allow this rule to operate in two contexts; namely, in open syllables and in closed syllables preceding glides. The global condition thus "collapses" two environments that would have to be separately stated in a non-global solution.

The analysis given by Kenstowicz and Kisseberth is not available to us, since our framework does not permit the use of global conditions. Not only would the derivation given above require a global condition on Vowel Deletion, but it also crucially involves the familiar global condition on Vowel Shortening to prevent it from operating on the output of Pre-glide Epenthesis to give the incorrect *[sdəsdinḱa].

We turn, then, to an alternate account of these forms in which global conditions play no role. We propose that the two environments collapsed by the global condition on Vowel Deletion represent, in fact, two rules: Vowel Deletion (15) and an independent rule of Pre-glide Schwa Deletion, which deletes schwas before a tautosyllabic glide. We formulate this rule as follows:

Figure 57

Pre-glide Schwa Deletion

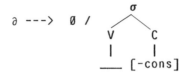

We have formulated Pre-glide Schwa Deletion in such a way that it applies only to vowels which have already undergone Vowel Reduction. This formulation makes the prediction that only vowels which have undergone Vowel Reduction will undergo Pre-glide Schwa Deletion, a prediction which is true. It will be recalled that an analogous argument for including the reduced vowel ∂ in the structural description of a rule was given in our previous discussion of Vowel Deletion (cf. section 2.3 above). There we showed that this formulation of Vowel Deletion explained the following, apparently unrelated restrictions on the application of the rule:[11]

---

11. It was further noted that Vowel Reduction, and hence Vowel Deletion, does not apply in suffixes. We have been unable to find examples of this restriction bearing on the formulation of Pre-glide Schwa Deletion.

Figure 58

a. Vowel Deletion never applies in initial syllables.

b. Vowel Deletion never applies to the second vowel of bisyllabic roots (cf. discussion of (10)).

c. Vowel Deletion may be exceptionally blocked in the context of either of the two 'intensive' formatives of class 6, $/C_0VC_0/$ or $/C_0VVC_0/$. (These are reduplications of the following syllables.)

These three restrictions hold for Pre-glide Schwa Deletion as well. This is illustrated in the following forms, in which the reduced vowel of the surface schwa-glide sequences is not created by Vowel Reduction, but by the late rule of Low Vowel Raising mentioned in footnote 1, Chapter 4.

Figure 59

a. (i) spə́wta	/spáw + otn + a/	'poisons someone'	D,387
(ii) stə́yLa	/stayLa + a/	'gathers food'	D,393
b. (i) qajə́ym?əm	/qájaym + ?m/	'manzanita'	D,326
(ii) sidyə́ykȧ	/sidyáyk + a/	'rejoices'	D,365
c. (i) ṅáṅo:qṅə́wqḱa	/ṅa + CVCC + ṅáwG + ḱa/	'little throats'	D,275
(ii) ?iwṅə́wṅa	/?í + CCV + awṅa + a/	'are cornered'	D,52

These examples show that the same considerations which motivated mention of the reduced vowel ə in the statement of Vowel Deletion carry over to the statement of Pre-glide Schwa Deletion. The examples in (59a) show that Pre-glide Schwa Deletion does not apply in the first syllable of a word. (59b) shows that Pre-glide Schwa Deletion does not affect the second vowel of a bisyllabic root. Finally, (59c) shows that the 'intensive' formative may block Vowel Reduction (and hence Pre-glide Schwa Deletion) in the immediately following morpheme.

Pre-glide Schwa Deletion, as we have formulated it, creates long vowels from underlying vowel-glide sequences. For example, "little heart" is derived in the following way:

Figure 60

Pre-glide Schwa Deletion deletes the schwa preceding the tautosyllabic glide, leaving an unoccupied V position in syllable structure. To this the non-consonantal segment /y/ reassociates under the Association Conventions of Chapter 3, as illustrated by the dashed line in the output. The resulting configuration describes a long vowel. This long vowel will not undergo Vowel Shortening under the assumption that Pre-glide Schwa Deletion is ordered later.

Our analysis assumes that the lengthening of the underlying glides in examples like those in (54) is not the result of Pre-glide Epenthesis (as in Kenstowicz and Kisseberth's analysis), but of a later rule that we have called Pre-glide Schwa Deletion. As further evidence that this is true, observe the following forms:

Figure 61

a.   ?i:Lo:nət   /?i + ?i + eLWn + at/   'put objects onto!'   D,128
b.   qiqo:hka   /qi + qi + Wk + a/   'snarl at' (distr.)   D,320

These forms illustrate a consistent difference between the outputs of

Pre-glide Epenthesis and Pre-glide Schwa Deletion when the glide in question is voiceless. Example (61a) illustrates the application of Pre-glide Epenthesis. Notice that as a result of the rule of Deglottalization/Deaspiration ((32) of Chapter 4), the underlying voiceless glide shows up as a voiced vowel. (62b) illustrates Pre-glide Schwa Deletion. In this case we see that the underlying voiceless glide surfaces as a diphthong consisting of a long vowel followed by [h]. If Pre-glide Epenthesis had been involved in the derivation of this latter form, it would have eliminated all evidence of the underlying voiceless glide. Hence, it must be concluded that the rule operating here as well as in forms like (54) is distinct from the rule of Pre-glide Epenthesis and is crucially ordered after the rule of Deglottalization/Deaspiration.

We have shown, therefore, that the deletion rule involved in the derivation of the examples in (54) is not subject to a global condition. In this case, unlike the previous one, the global condition in question does not follow from the limitations of the linear framework itself, but seems to have resulted from an illicit collapsing of two rules, our (15) and (57). While both of these rules delete schwas, they cannot be collapsed, since one rule feeds Vowel Shortening and the other rule counterfeeds it.

This concludes our solution to the problem posed by the long vowels in Klamath. We have demonstrated that the syllable-based theory presented here allows a straightforward solution which does not need to resort to global conditions on phonological rules.

5.5 Excursus: Remarks on a Non-cyclic Alternative

In a recent study, Feinstein and Vago (1981) propose an analysis of Klamath phonology which does not make use of the cycle, and which offers a different account of the epenthesis, vowel reduction and vowel deletion processes that we have examined in the last two chapters. The purpose of these authors, in their words, is "(a) to show that Kean's (1974) analysis is internally flawed, and (b) that a viable non-cyclic analysis of her data is possible" (p.119). We examine the adequacy of the Feinstein and Vago analysis here.

Apart from the fact that they assume non-cyclic derivations, Feinstein and Vago differ primarily from our analysis in the following respects. First, the effect of the rule of Sonorant Cluster Epenthesis (cf. Feinstein and Vago (27)) is duplicated by a rule of Sonorant Syllabification (Feinstein and Vago (20)) accomplishing much the same effect, but ordered before Vowel Deletion. This rule has no counterpart in our analysis. Second, Vowel Deletion (Feinstein and Vago (18)) is formulated as a much more general rule than ours, deleting any short vowel (and not just schwa) occurring in a noninitial syllable either before a glide, or in an open syllable, or (if in absolute morpheme-initial position) unconditionally. Third, Vowel Reduction is ordered after Vowel Deletion and Glottal Lengthening, instead of before, as in our analysis. Fourth, Vowel Shortening, which is not formalized, is informally stated as follows (142, note 2): "in certain contexts long vowels predictably undergo a rule of shortening." This rule does not distinguish between the three types of long vowels illustrated in (1) above. We take up the last two points only since these are the most significant.

Feinstein and Vago (144, note 12) order Vowel Reduction after their version of Vowel Deletion and Glottal Lengthening in order to achieve a noncyclic derivation of the form [soso:yo:qa] 'shave themselves' (distr.) (cf. our (34c) and the derivation in (36)). Their derivation is as follows:

Figure 62

/so + so + ?o + yo:q + a/	Underlying Representation
so + so + ? + yo:q + a	Vowel Deletion (right to left iterative)
so + so: + yo:q + a	Glottal Lengthening
n/a	Vowel Reduction
soso:yo:qa	output

If, in this derivation, Vowel Reduction were allowed to precede Vowel Deletion, and hence Glottal Lengthening, it would incorrectly reduce the vowel of the reflexive/reciprocal prefix (the second prefix in the underlying representation), giving *[sosəyoːʔa]. However, the ordering assumed by Feinstein and Vago can be independently shown to be incorrect. First, we have seen that Vowel Deletion applies only to those vowels which are eligible for Vowel Reduction. This relationship can be captured by requiring Vowel Deletion to apply only to schwas introduced by Vowel Reduction, as Kean (1974) first suggested, but remains unaccounted for in Feinstein and Vago's approach. Second, this ordering is demonstrably wrong in the case of bisyllabic verb roots, as we already saw in (11), repeated below:

Figure 63

/sni + nkililk̓ + a/
sni + nklilk̓ + a   Vowel Deletion
*sni + nkləlk̓ + a   Vowel Reduction

The correct output, as we have seen, is [sninklilka], which can be obtained if Vowel Reduction precedes Vowel Deletion in the ordering. But given this ordering, there is no noncyclic derivation of [sosoːyoːʔa].

Secondly, a noncyclic analysis cannot derive any of the remaining forms given in Section 3 of this chapter. For example, the form [qbəqptiːwəpk] 'will wrap their legs around' (distr.) must be incorrectly derived as follows:

Figure 64

/qba + qbaty̓ + wabg/   Underlying Representation
n/a   Vowel Deletion
qba + qbatiː + wabg   Glide Vocalization
qba + qbətiː + wabg   Vowel Reduction

   * qbəqbə́ti:wəpk   other rules

Vowel Deletion will be inapplicable until Glide Vocalization has applied; but Vowel Deletion must be ordered first, in Feinstein and Vago's approach, to account for forms like [swiso:nis] (20aii). Thus, there is no way of eliminating the initial vowel of the stem.

  Most importantly, the Feinstein and Vago analysis does not offer a solution to the problem raised by Vowel Shortening, which in their analysis must retain its global condition. This follows from the fact that Vowel Deletion, generalized to apply before glides, will neutralize the crucial distinction between underlying /CGC/ sequences and underlying /CVGC/ sequences. The following incorrect derivation of [pnipno:pća] 'blow out' (distr.) illustrates this:[12]

---

12. As a further remark, it should be pointed out that neither Feinstein and Vago's analysis, nor ours, provides a straightforward account of the following forms:

a.	(i)	s?ə́ywə́kta	/s?aywg + otn + a/	'knows'	D,342
	(ii)	hahə́s?i:wgis	/ha + has + s?aywg + y + s/	'teacher' (distr.)	D,342
b.	(i)	?iwi:Ga	/?i + iwyG + a/	'puts pl. objects into a container'	D,176
	(ii)	?i?o:yGa	/?i + ?i + iwyG + a/	'put pl. objects into a container' (distr.)	D,176

In the second member of each pair, we would have expected the rightmost member of each underlying glide sequence to vocalize by Pre-glide Epenthesis; we observe, however, that the leftmost glide vocalizes in both cases. Feinstein and Vago suggest that these forms undergo a subcase of Pre-glide Epenthesis (their "Vocalization"), applicable to the context /...CGGC + .../. However, they were able to find no more forms motivating this subcase. Consequently, the linguistic evidence for this analysis is very meager. We suggest, rather, that whatever the historical motivation for these two forms, they are best treated as exceptional forms whose exceptionality consists in the fact that the glide sequences in question are fully syllabified and tautosyllabic in the lexicon. On this assumption, our rules will apply correctly to derive the surface forms.

Figure 65

/pni + pniw + abc' + a/   Underlying Representation

pni + pnw + bc' + a   Vowel Deletion

pni + pno: + bc' + a   Glide Vocalization

n/a   Vowel Reduction

pni + pno + bc' + a   Vowel Shortening

*pnipnopc'a   other rules

5.6 Conclusion

Merely to show that a given analysis of a certain body of data is incorrect is not generally of theoretical interest. What is instructive about the reanalysis of Klamath that we have given here, assuming it is correct in relevant respects, is the fact that the global rule condition proposed by Kisseberth was not the result of misanalysis, but rather followed from the logical structure of the standard theory. Within this framework, there was no non-ad-hoc way of expressing the proper condition on the applicability of Vowel Shortening without reference to earlier stages in the derivation. Given the strong independent reasons for wishing to exclude global conditions of this type, this consequence resulted in an irresoluble anomaly in the theory of generative phonology of the period. This anomaly, being without a solution, was simply suppressed from later discussion; indeed, no recent published article on Klamath makes any reference to the problem. While the solution turns out to be trivially simple from the standpoint of the present theory of the syllable, what is interesting is that this model was not developed in order to deal with the problem of globality as such, but with totally unrelated problems. This result offers welcome confirmation of our theory, which is all the more forceful in that it comes from such an unexpected source.

References

Abercrombie, D., <u>Elements of General Phonetics</u>, Aldine and Atherton, Chicago, 1967.

Algeo, J., "What Consonant Clusters are Possible?," <u>Word</u> 29.3, 206-224, 1978.

Anderson, J. and C. Jones, "Three Theses Concerning Phonological Representations," <u>Journal of Linguistics</u> 10, 1-26, 1974.

Barker, M.A.R., <u>Klamath Dictionary</u>, University of California Press Publication in Linguistics 31, University of California Press, Berkeley, 1963.

Barker, M.A.R., <u>Klamath Grammar</u>, University of California Press Publication in Linguistics 32, University of California Press, Berkeley, 1964.

Basbøll, H., "The Phonological Syllable with Special Reference to Danish," ARIPUC 8, 38-128, Institute of Phonetics, University of Copenhagen, 1974.

Brooks, M. Z., "On Polish Affricates," <u>Word</u> 20, 207-10, 1965.

Brown, R. and D. McNeill, "The 'Tip of the Tongue' Phenomenon," <u>Journal of Verbal Learning and Verbal Behavior</u> 5.4, 325-37, 1966.

Browne, W. "Slavic -<u>ba</u> and English *<u>slil</u>: Two Persistent Constraints," unpublished manuscript, Cornell University, 1981.

Campbell, L., "Phonological Features: Problems and Proposals," <u>Language</u> 50, 52-65, 1974.

Campbell, L. "The Psychological and Social Reality of Finnish Vowel Harmony," in R.M. Vago, ed., <u>Issues in Vowel Harmony</u>, John Benjamins, B.V., Amsterdam, 245-270, 1980.

Chomsky, N. and M. Halle, Sound Pattern of English, Harper and Row, New York, 1968.

Church, K. and R. Patil, "Coping with Syntactic Ambiguity or How to Put the Block in the Box on the Table, "Laboratory of Computer Science Publication No. MIT/LCS/TM-216, MIT, 1982.

Clements, G.N., "Syllable and Mora in Luganda," unpublished manuscript, Harvard University, 1978.

Clements, G.N., "Akan Vowel Harmony: a Nonlinear Analysis," in G.N. Clements, ed., Harvard Studies in Phonology 2, Indiana University Linguistics Club, Bloomington, Indiana, 1981.

Clements, G.N. "Compensatory Lengthening and Consonant Gemination in Luganda," paper presented at the Minifestival on Compensatory Lengthening, Harvard University, May 1982.

Clements, G.N. and K.C. Ford, "Kikuyu Tone Shift and its Synchronic Consequences," Linguistic Inquiry, 10.2, 179-210, 1979.

Clements, G.N. and S.J. Keyser, "The Hierarchical Nature of the Klamath Syllable," unpublished manuscript, Harvard and MIT, 1980.

Clements, G.N. and S.J. Keyser, "A Three-Tiered Theory of the Syllable," Occasional Paper No. 19, The Center for Cognitive Science, MIT, 1981.

Davidsen-Nielsen, N., "Syllabification in English Words with Medial sp, st, sk," Journal of Phonetics 2.1, 15-45, 1974.

Elimelech, B., A Tonal Grammar of Etsako, University of California Press, Berkeley, 1978.

Feinstein, M. and R. Vago, "Non-evidence for the Segmental Cycle in Klamath," in D.L. Goyvaerts, ed. Phonology in the 1980's, Story-Scientia, Ghent, 119-145, 1981.

Fouché, P., Traité de pronunciation française, Klincksieck, Paris, 1959.

Fromkin, V., "The Nonanomalous Nature of Anomalous Utterances," Language 47, 27-52, 1971.

Fudge, E.C. "Syllables," Journal of Linguistics 5, 1969.

Gaatone, D., "Phonologie abstraite et phonologie concrète: à propos de h aspiré en français," Lingvisticae Investigationes 2, 3-22, 1978.

Goldsmith, J. "An Autosegmental Typology of Tone: and How Japanese Fits In," in E. Kaisse, J. Hankamer, eds., NELS 5, Department of Linguistics, Harvard University, 172-182, 1974.

Goldsmith, J., Autosegmental Phonology, doctoral dissertation, MIT, 1976 [published by Garland Publishing Company, New York, 1979].

Greenberg, J. and J. J. Jenkins, "Studies in the Psychological Correlates of the Sound System of American English," Word 20.2, 157-177, 1964.

Halle, M., "Formal versus Functional Considerations in Phonology," in B. Kachru, ed., Linguistics in the Seventies: Directions and Prospects, Studies in the Linguistic Sciences 8, 2. Department of Linguistics, University of Illinois, Urbana, 123-134, 1978.

Halle, M. and J.-R. Vergnaud, "Metrical Phonology (A Fragment of a Draft)," unpublished manuscript, 1979.

Halle, M. and J.-R. Vergnaud, "Three Dimensional Phonology," Journal of Linguistic Research, 1.1, 83-105, 1980.

Harris, J.W., "Sequences of Vowels in Spanish," Linguistic Inquiry 1.1, 129-34, 1970.

Harris, J.W., "Nonconcatenative Morphology and Spanish Plurals," Journal of Linguistic Research 1, 15-31, 1980.

Harris, J.W., Syllable Structure and Stress in Spanish: a Nonlinear Approach, Linguistic Inquiry Monograph No. 8, MIT Press, 1983.

Haugen, E., "The Syllable in Linguistic Description," in M. Halle, H.G. Lunt, and H. McClean, eds., For Roman Jakobson, The Hague: Mouton, 213-21, 1956.

Hoard, J.E., On the Foundations of Phonological Theory, doctoral dissertation, University of Washington, Seattle, 1967.

Hockett, C.F. "Problems of Morphemic Analysis," Language 23, 321-43, 1947.

Hooper, J.B., "The Syllable in Phonological Theory," Language 48, 525-540, 1972.

Hutchinson, S.P. "Spanish Vowel Sandhi," in A. Bruck, R.A. Fox, M.W. La Galy, eds., Papers from the Parasession on Natural Phonology, Chicago Linguistic Society, Chicago. Illinois, 184-192, 1974.

Ingria, R., "Compensatory Lengthening as a Metrical Phenomenon," Linguistic Inquiry 11.3, 465-495, 1980.

Jakobson, R., Selected Writings 1: Phonological Studies, second expanded edition, Mouton & Co., The Hague, 1962.

Jakobson, R., Child Language, Aphasia and Phonological Universals, Mouton & Co., The Hague, 1968.

Kahn, D., Syllable-based Generalizations in English Phonology, doctoral dissertation, MIT, 1976 [published by Garland Publishing Company, New York, 1980].

Kean, M.-L., "Nonglobal Rules in Klamath Phonology," MIT Quarterly Progress Report No. 108, 288-310, 1973.

Kean, M.-L., "The Strict Cycle in Phonology," Linguistic Inquiry 5, 179-203, 1974.

Kenstowicz, M. and C. Kisseberth, Topics in Phonological Theory, Academic Press, New York, 1977.

Keyser, S.J. and P. Kiparsky, "Syllable Structure in Finnish Phonology," unpublished manuscript, MIT, 1982.

Kiparsky, P., "Phonological Representations," in O. Fujimura, ed., Three Dimensions of Linguistic Theory, TEC Co., Tokyo, 1973.

Kiparsky, P., "Metrical Structure Assignment is Cyclic," Linguistic Inquiry, 10.3, 521-41, 1979.

Kiparsky, P., "Remarks on the Metrical Structure of the Syllable," in Wolfgang U. Dressler, O.E. Pfeiffer and J.R. Rennison, eds., Phonologica 1980, Akten der Vierten Internationalen Phonologie-Tagung, Wien, 29 Juni-2 Juli 1980 [published 1981].

Kiparsky, P., "Lexical Morphology and Phonology," in I.-S. Yang, ed., Linguistics in the Morning Calm, Seoul, Hanshin, 1982.

Kisseberth, C., "On the Alternation of Vowel Length in Klamath: A Global Rule," in M. Kenstowicz and C. Kisseberth, eds., Issues in Phonological Theory, Mouton, The Hague, 1973a.

Kisseberth, C., "The 'Strict Cyclicity' Principle: The Klamath Evidence," in C. Kisseberth, ed., Studies in Generative Phonology. Papers in Linguistics Monograph Series No. 3, Linguistic Research Incorporated, Edmonton, Alberta, 1973b.

Kisseberth, C.W., "Displaced Tones in Digo (Part 2)," Studies in the Linguistic Sciences 11.1, 73-120, Spring, 1981.

Klatt, D.M., "Vowel Lengthening is Syntactically Determined in a Connected Discourse," Journal of Phonetics 3, 129-40, 1975.

Klausenburger, J., "French Linking Phenomena," Language 54,1, 21-40, 1978.

Kornfilt, J., "Long Vowels in Turkish in a Three-Dimensional Model," paper presented to the 57th Annual Meeting of the Linguistic Society of America, San Diego, California, 1982.

Kurylowicz, J., "Contribution à la théorie de la syllabe," Biuletyn polskiego towarzystwa jezykoznawczego 8. 80-114, 1948.

Laughren, M., "Tone in Zulu Nouns," in G.N. Clements and J. Goldsmith, eds., Autosegmental Studies in Bantu Tone, Foris Publications, Dordrecht-Holland, in press.

Lauritsen, M., "Phonetic Study of the Danish stød," POLA Reports 7 (second series), Phonology Laboratory, University of California, Berkeley, D1 D12, 1968.

Leben, W., "A Metrical Analysis of Length," Linguistic Inquiry, 11.3, 497-509, 1980.

Levin, L.S., "A Look at English Vowels," unpublished manuscript, MIT, 1981.

Lewis, G.L., Turkish Grammar, Oxford University Press, London, 1967.

Liberman, M., The Intonational System of English, doctoral dissertation, MIT, 1975.

Liberman, M. and A. Prince, "On Stress and Linguistic Rhythm," Linguistic Inquiry 8.2, 249-336, 1977.

Malmberg, B., Phonétique Française, Hermods, Malmo, Sweden, 1972.

Martin, W.A., K. Church and R. Patil, "Preliminary Analysis of a Breadth-First Parsing Algorithm: Theoretical and Experimental Results," Laboratory of Computer Science Publication No. MIT/LCS/TR-261, MIT, 1981.

Martinet, A., "La phonologie du mot en danois," BSLP 38, 169-266, 1937.

Mascaró, J., Catalan Phonology and the Phonological Cycle, doctoral dissertation, MIT, 1976 [distributed by the Indiana University Linguistics Club, Bloomington, Indiana].

McCarthy, J., "On Stress and Syllabification," Linguistic Inquiry, 10, 443-65, 1979a.

McCarthy, J., Formal Problems in Semitic Phonology and Morphology, doctoral dissertation, MIT, 1979b.

McCarthy, J., "A Prosodic Theory of Nonconcatenative Morphology," Linguistic Inquiry, 12.3, 373-418, 1981.

McCarthy, J., "A Prosodic Account of Arabic Broken Plurals," in Ivan R. Dihoff, ed., Current Approaches to African Linguistics, vol. 1, Foris Publications, Dordrecht-Holland, in press.

Menn, L., "An Autosegmental Approach to Child Phonology: First Explorations," in G.N. Clements, ed., Harvard Studies in Phonology, Vol. 1, Department of Linguistics, Harvard University, Cambridge, Mass., 315-33, 1977.

Menn, L., "Phonological Units in Beginning Speech," in Alan Bell and J.B. Hooper, eds., Syllables and Segments, North-Holland, Amsterdam, 157-171, 1978.

Michelson, K., "Stress, Epenthesis and Syllable Structure in Mohawk," in G.N. Clements, ed., Harvard Studies in Phonology, 2, Indiana University Linguistics Club, Bloomington, Indiana, 311-53, 1981.

Milner, J.C., "French Truncation Rule," in Quarterly Progress Report of the Research Laboratory of Electronics No. 86, MIT, 273-83, 1967.

Milner, J.-C., Arguments Linguistiques, Paris, Mame, 1973.

Napoli, D.J. and M. Nespor, "The Syntax of Word-Initial
    Consonant Gemination in Italian," Language, 55.4, 812-41,
    1979.

Navarro Tomás, T., Métrica Espanola, Ediciones Guardarrama,
    Madrid, 1972.

Odden, D., "A Nonlinear Approach to Vowel Length in
    Kimatuumbi," unpublished manuscript, Yale University,
    forthcoming.

Petersen, P. R., "An Instrumental Study of the Danish 'stød'," in
    ARIPUC 7, 195-234, Institute of Phonetics, University of
    Copenhagen, 1973.

Pike, K. and E. Pike, "Immediate Constituents of Mazateco
    Syllables," IJAL 13, 78-91, 1947.

Reyes, R., Studies in Chicano Spanish, doctoral dissertation,
    Harvard University, Cambridge, Mass., 1976.

Roca, I. "Explorations on Extrametricality," unpublished
    manuscript, MIT, 1982.

Schane, S., French Phonology and Morphology, Research
    Monograph No. 45, MIT Press, Cambridge, Mass., 1968.

Schane, S., Generative Phonology, Prentice-Hall, Englewood
    Cliffs, N.J., 1973.

Schane, S., "L'emploi des frontières de mot en français," in B. de
    Cornulier and F. Dell, eds., Etudes de Phonologie Française,
    Editions du Centre National de la Recherche Scientifique,
    Paris, l33-147, 1978.

Selkirk, E.O., "French Liaison and the X-bar Notation," Linguistic
    Inquiry, 5, 573-90, 1974.

Selkirk, E.O., "On Prosodic Structure and its Relation to Syntactic
    Structure," paper presented to the Conference on Mental
    Representation in Phonology, November, 1978.

Selkirk, E.O., "The Role of Prosodic Categories in English Word Stress," Linguistic Inquiry 11.3. 563-605, 1980.

Selkirk, E.O. and J.-R. Vergnaud, "How Abstract is French Phonology?" Foundations of Language 10, 249-54, 1973.

Sezer, E., "The k/Ø Alternation in Turkish," in G.N. Clements, ed., Harvard Studies in Phonology, Vol. 2, Indiana University Linguistics Club, Bloomington, Indiana, 1981.

Sezer, E., "An Autosegmental Analysis of Compensatory Lengthening in Turkish," paper delivered at the Minifestival on Compensatory Lengthening, Harvard University, May 1982.

Shockey, L., "Perceptual Text of a Phonological Rule," Status Report on Speech Research SR-50, Haskins Laboratories, New Haven, Connecticut, 147-150, 1977.

Smith, N., The Acquisition of Phonology: A Case Study, Cambridge University Press, Cambridge, England, 1973.

Stemann, I., Danish: A Practical Reader, H. Hagerup Publishers, Copenhagen, 1965.

Steriade, D. Greek Prosodies and the Nature of Syllabification, unpublished doctoral dissertation, MIT, 1982.

Ter Mors, C., "Klamath ə-Insertion in Empty Syllabic Nuclei," paper presented to the 56th Annual Meeting of the LSA, New York City, 1981a.

Ter Mors, C., "Directional Syllabification," unpublished manuscript, Rijksuniversiteit Groningen, The Netherlands, 1981b.

Thomas, L., Klamath Vowel Alternations and the Segmental Cycle, doctoral dissertation, University of Massachusetts, Amherst [distributed by the Graduate Student Association, Department of Linguistics, University of Massachusetts, Amherst 1974].

Thráinsson, H. "On the Phonology of Icelandic Preaspiration," Nordic Journal of Linguistics 1.1, 3-54, 1978.

Tranel, B., Concreteness In Generative Phonology, University of California Press, Berkeley, 1981

Trubetzkoy, N.S., Grundzüge der Phonologie, Vandenhoeck and Ruprecht in Gottingen, 1958.

Vennemann, T. "An Outline of Universal Phonology (Preliminary Version)," unpublished manuscript, Universität München, 1979.

Welmers, W.E. African Language Structures, University of California Press, Berkeley, 1973.

White, R., Klamath Phonology. Studies in Linguistics and Language Learning 12, Department of Linguistics, University of Washington, Seattle, 1973.

Williams, E. "Underlying Tone in Margi and Igbo," Linguistic Inquiry 7.3, 463-84, 1976.

Yip, M. "Reduplication and C-V Skeleta in Chinese Secret Languages," Linguistic Inquiry 13.4, 637-661, 1982.